How T
America

by
Bruce Jenvey

Coven Books
www.facebook.com/CovenBooks

Published by
Coven Books © 2019
ISBN: 9781082432149

On The Cover:
Cover Art created by John Kenneth Bruce
All Rights Reserved
Cover Art © 2019 by Coven Books

www.facebook.com/CovenBooks

Dedication

To Norman Rockwell
Who told the story of life in these United States, one picture at a time…

Foreword/Warning

This book is going to be politically incorrect as hell, in fact, as politically incorrect as I can make it. In the pages that follow, I will offend literally dozens of groups, movements, organizations, sects, cults, regions, clubs, unions, teams, tea-groups, troops, brotherhoods, gangs, mobs, and even more disaffected individuals whom have fought very hard for many years for the 'progress' they have made. And if I miss anyone, I apologize. Just know I was thinking about you, too.

I assure you, by the last page, everyone will have had their motivation to scream 'foul,' 'unfounded,' and burn me in effigy. But perhaps, just maybe, you may find some unity, some common ground between you, as you stir the tar pot for my feathers, together.

Detractors will say I have some of my facts wrong, and then use that to discredit the entire work. Some will scream and shout obscenities and feel it justifies vandalizing whole city blocks while concealing their identities. Question the source of these critics and ask yourself, what side are they truly on? Is it just a group you sympathize with, align with, or cheer for? Or is it really *your* side? "Your side" meaning the side you sit down with at the dinner table and share the day's events and labors.

Remember above all else, this is not a "plan." These are only opinions, ideas, thought starters, questions for you to consider and then say "Why?" or "Why not?" It only means you do not accept things as they are and if nothing else, that you should consider *all* options before you resign yourself to a fate others have decided for you.

You will be tempted to toss/burn this book several times before you finish, but if you do, you will only hear about the section you hadn't read yet from someone else. Then you'll need to buy it again. Some people may have to purchase this book five or six times before they reach the last page. But that's okay. I need the money…

—Bruce Jenvey

Part One

What's Wrong?

You can't have a discussion about how to fix anything unless you can agree that it is indeed broken. And then you need to come to some sort of partial consensus as to what it is that's wrong. Blessed is the fool today who can look about him and say, "The state of the Union is great! Let's not change a thing!" I know as a fact, there are many who would disagree with that assessment and while they may not agree on what needs to be changed and how, they know we ain't livin' in no Garden of Eden here. I'll try *not* to make this section sound like some laundry list, bitch session, but I'm afraid I see much that needs to change and our time to do so may be running out. Again, these are only my own personal opinions and any offense you take from this section is your own. But come on! It'll be fun!

Income Disparity is perhaps the greatest, most singly responsible cause for all our troubles and issues. "One" can cause "another" and yet "another" creating a "situation" that rapidly deteriorates in to a "condition" and then it's all downhill from there. It is probably true that 'money is the root all evil,' so why shouldn't it be at the root of all our problems as well?

Now, I don't want to sound like a Bernie Sanders clone because I am most definitely *not*. But he has certainly targeted this flaw in our society today. Bear in mind, *any* successful leader, politician, dictator, or savior *always* starts by indentifying and isolating a problem most of us can agree upon, and then uses that anger, that angst, that surrounds that problem to advance his position with the people. The difference is always in how that leader proposes to *solve* the problem. That's what sets them apart. Bernie Sanders does not own Income Disparity as an issue. The vast majority of us suffer from it so we get to talk about it, too!

Now, exactly what *is* Income Disparity? It's the difference between the smallest paychecks and the largest. It's the difference between the stock boy's take home pay and the CEO's. Everyone expects the boss to make

[7]

more. It's a fact of life and has been the norm since the beginning of time. There will *always* be Income Disparity. But the question is 'how much is too much?'

How can any corporation encourage their rank and file employees to apply for food stamps to get by, yet pass out twenty-eight million dollar bonuses to their top executives? Where does anyone get the disposable income to offer a six-and-a-half million dollar bribe to get their kid into a college he doesn't deserve, and at the same time tell the cashiers there is nothing left in the budget for raises? That is when Income Disparity becomes a *problem*... and not just because people are pissed off. It creates an imbalance in the cash flow and can actually stagnate an economy.

Eventually, in extreme cases, that always leads to violence in the streets and revolution in the capitals. But in even the 'best case' scenarios, it creates a lower class completely dependent on an upper class that eventually, it will be no longer able to support. It's like playing Monopoly and you have *all* the cash... but none of the property. Eventually, you *will* go broke.

That's what happened in the 1920s and 30s and obviously we haven't learned our lessons. Many people believe the 'sum-it-up-in-a-paragraph' history book explanation that the Great Depression started on one sunny day in late October, 1929. We all went to bed rich one night and by the end of the next day, we were all broke. I'm afraid it's not that simple.

Our vision of the 1920s has always been a time of great excess, mansions, wild parties, fancy cars and 'The Great Gatsby' way of life. It was for the most elite Americans. Being the 'beautiful people,' they captured the headlines and photographers' attentions and therefore are the ones we remember. But the truth is, the working classes had struggled all the way through the 20s as one by one, mills were shuttered, quarries closed and family farms were lost to the banks. Due to Income Disparity, their way of life had become 'unviable' in the new scheme of things. They could no longer make enough money doing what they had been doing to meet their basic needs.

The economy dried-up, from the bottom up as all the cash flowed to the top and just didn't return to complete the cycle. As with any building that has rotted timbers in its foundation, one day, it started to collapse. But it didn't happen over-night. It took weeks and months. Just like the Titanic, it may have been doomed the moment it hit the iceberg, but it took over two-and-a-half hours to slip below the surface… and then, the better part of a half hour to find the bottom! The Great Depression really began in the early 1920s and took nearly a decade for everyone to notice… and it all started with Income Disparity.

How does that relate to our current situation? Because it's happening again! In fact, Income Disparity is even greater today than it was back in the 20s. But now, with the social programs and safety nets we have put on the system and our society, things may just crash in slow motion compared to back then. We have enough guy wires on this vertical tower of an economy that many believe it could *never* fall over and play dead again. But it can, and it is! Just is, *this* time, Income Disparity is attacking the foundation from the core, outward and we need to recognize the basic symptoms.

The problem today is much like back then. The cost of things we need, and should *reasonably* aspire to own, have ballooned much faster than even the rate of inflation and have outstripped our ability to pay for them. Well, at least for some of us. But this did not happen to everyone at once, mind you. It took years, decades even, and when it started back in the late 1960s and early 70s, we all felt a little sorry for the people at the very bottom of the food chain who were having problems providing this or that for their families. We all made some provision. We kicked in a little more to the collection plates and the telethons, and in some cases, legislation and government programs were initiated and then continually expanded. We all felt better that we had done our jobs as concerned American citizens… and then went about our own business, secretly feeling that some of that problem would be resolved if those folks would only go out and get a job.

But somehow, the help we gave was never enough. Things didn't get better for these Americans and if anything, it seemed there were more and more of them over time. That so-called 'poverty line' kept creeping higher and higher until what was once a distant concern could now be seen from our own front porches. Like a slowly sinking ship, those bilge rats kept crawling out of the woodwork as dry space below decks became more and more sparse. Then, they started fighting among themselves for what air remained. Before we realized it, we, ourselves, were surrounded by those same rats and could feel our own tails and whiskers starting to grow as the walls closed in.

You can laugh at this, laugh at the analogy and many will even laugh at the idea itself that this has indeed become a reality. But think about this:

[9]

Let's do a little time travel back to those 1960s. Back then, people complained about taxes, and the skyrocketing cost of living that never seem to be reflected in their paystubs. That's true. I was there and lived through that. But those people had no idea how good they had it by today's standards.

In 1968, it was possible for a shop worker, making a steady wage of four dollars per hour, to support his family... by himself. Maybe his car wasn't new, and maybe he did his own break jobs in the front yard with the help of a son. Maybe they didn't eat steak. His wife... who was a housewife still at that point, had to be prudent with her household budget. But if they were careful, they could live on one income. She could raise the kids, and if they were *real* frugal, they could send their kids off to college... one at a time. It was the American Dream of its day and done so the next generation would have it better than they did.

What started in the 1960s in the lowest income groups, slowly spread upward through the tax brackets as the years went on. Women were financially *compelled* to re-enter the work force. In memory of their Rosie the Riveter heritage and in the midst of a booming economy, they went back to work out of necessity to keep the family afloat.

There are two things to note here: First, in this era, the husband and wife still tended to be on the same team and pulled together for common goals. After all, this was about family, *their* family. But that *other* thing to note was not so positive and raised the question, "so who's watching the kids?" There were a lot of answers to that question and while they were justified and rationalized at the time, none of them were good answers. Generally, we heard things like: "The neighbor lady keeps an eye on things," (from the comfort of her living room chair with the drapes drawn so she can see the TV screen). "The older one keeps an eye on the young ones," (as long as she's not too busy making unsupervised decisions of her own). And I always liked "It's only a couple of hours until one or the other of us gets home. How much trouble can they get into in just a couple of hours?" Generally, due to the cost of child care even back then, it often meant no one was watching the kids at *all*... Children who raise themselves generally do a poor job of it and then take those skills into adulthood with them. And we've been doing that for two generations now!

Not to sound sexist in the least (although I personally know a few feminists who are now burning this book and will soon be adding to my

[10]

royalty check with a re-purchase), but I like to think there is no one better suited to see to the children, to nurture them, to teach those daily lessons of right, wrong, responsibility, family commitment, and *home*, (yes, HOME is a lesson) than Mom herself. Yes there will be exceptions, yes there are alternatives. But, raising your kids to be of the same heart and mind as you cannot be done by strangers. If you want them to be like you and share your values, make what you consider to be the 'right' decisions, you have to raise them yourself and tend to their needs *daily*.

But we lost that with the need for dual incomes and over time, that need for dual incomes overtook more and more American families. I remember as a kid, having friends who would invite me over after school. When I arrived, I would discover their mom was not home like mine was and I saw firsthand how much trouble kids can get into in just a couple of hours. You want to know where disrespect starts? And I mean disrespect for siblings at first, then the parents, then the school and then the whole damn system. You know where that starts? You want to know where grades start to slide taking opportunities with them? Ever wonder where your extra cigarettes went or why the whiskey bottle doesn't look as dark as it used to? That all started in those two hours after school before Mom got home from her shift. I remember thinking at the time that this kid or that kid was bound for trouble… maybe even prison. Turns out I was right twice over just a decade or so down the road.

So that slippery slope began in the 60s and early 70s and while it was creeping further and further up the ranks, it spread out. With every child's failure, every shortfall in the budget, every missed schedule and every sarcastic remark, tensions grew. And as tensions grew, relationships failed. Now, the problems were compounded by splitting the incomes, parents that couldn't peacefully be in the same room at the same time, and kids that quickly learned to play one off the other in the confusion and lack of communication. And somewhere above the din, there were other women shouting, "You don't need a man to make your life complete, you can do all of it by yourself!" and lawyers who said "I can fight her for what's rightfully yours, just give me more of that money you don't have…"

Let me set the Feminists at ease… sort of. I truly believe there are women out there today who can indeed do anything a man can do. I have worked with such women, I have worked *for* such women. Those that are

[11]

focused on the job and *not* on the idea that they are 'the woman who has now arrived' in this job, do very well. I truly believe they should receive equal pay for their efforts, I truly do.

But I have also seen women trying to be corporate giants *and* Super-Mom of the year. And just like any Jack of All Trades, you tend to be master of none. Think about it, if fast-paced office jobs can leave men burned out and ready for that early grave, wouldn't it do the same to women? And now on top of that, add the stress and responsibility of raising the next successful generation. There is nothing wrong with a woman who chooses a corporate career path. Just as there is nothing wrong, or 'less,' about a woman who chooses motherhood and raising her children as her career path. Both are all-consuming, difficult jobs of equal importance. But my personal opinion is that a choice has to be made. However, the problems of Income Disparity all too often deprive us of the luxury of proper choices.

Marriages that managed to survive 'Dual Income, Part-Time Kids,' have had their own set of problems. As women climbed the corporate ladders and fought for equal pay (and yes, *still* fighting for equal pay), their careers demanded more and more of their time and their commitment, causing home life to be 'readjusted' yet again. With the financial ups and downs of more recent years, it has become a reality that some wives will earn more money than their husbands.

For some, this is another one of those 'adjustments' and somewhere in the process... it all became a competition. Husbands and wives were no longer pulling on the same end of the same rope for the benefit of the entire family. Now, we had created a subculture of men vs. women. Don't think that exists? Watch some TV commercials and then say you can't see it. Especially in products aimed at women, we see women gleefully outperforming men at the gym, in the marathon run, behind the wheel of a performance automobile. And now, even all our superheroes are becoming women. And on it goes. Somewhere in all that, we lost sight of the children.

Now, so far, we can blame Income Disparity for the collapse of the family unit. Requiring two bread winners creates tensions and shortcomings in the relationship. It leaves children with limited and inconsistent parenting, all resulting in even lower incomes and some very unpleasant children for the rest of society to deal with. But where is the *disparity* part of this equation? It's at the far other end of the pay scale.

How did this happen? Why did prices rise so fast? How did my income get outstripped? Why are cars so expensive? Why is a college education so out of reach for so many, without entering into lifelong debt? Why can't my kids own their own home?

It's actually pretty simple. Those prices ballooned out of reach because there were other people ready and willing to pay those higher prices. For whatever reasons, they could actually afford it. And the more they acquired, the easier it became to acquire more, and more. But when things go to the highest bidder, those at the bottom of the list often get outbid. The fact that there are people out there with the money to easily afford these things is the *disparity* in Income Disparity.

As I said before, everyone one expects the boss to make more. It's a fact of life and has been the norm since the beginning of time. But everyone also knows that there are companies with full-time employees on food stamps while upstairs, management is giving themselves those big fat bonuses. How? Because they can! And it all happened so slowly we didn't see it coming. But they had some help too, and we will address that in another section. So, don't burn this book (again) unless you are in a financial position to comfortably buy yourself another copy. But if you do, I thank you for that.

If you are an employer and haven't given your employees, *all* of them, a significant raise in the last five years, yet in that same time, you have bought yourself a new car or a new home, you are in the running for the Ebenezer Scrooge Awards this year! If it's been ten years and you bought yourself more than one car, and gave your old one to your kid to take to college, don't be surprised to find your employees secretly assembling an Ikea Guillotine in your stock room. And if you bought your kid a brand *new* car to take to college... you might find yourself at the 'head' of the test line. Yes, pun intended. This also holds true if you are a middle level executive and allowed top management to shower these things upon you while you watched those below you struggle. You, too, are part of the reason for Income Disparity.

The disparity side of this imbalance causes other issues as well. Principally, housing becomes difficult for the masses to afford. Has everyone noticed it seems like no one is building middle-class housing anymore? That's because there's no money in it for the builder. Not when he can build houses in a blossoming subdivision that all *start* in the 'Low $450ks." And that right there tells you how much those nicer ones will cost!

[13]

More and more, middle class families are being forced into smaller, pre-existing homes that are still, slowly being priced out of their reach. The problem with pre-existing homes, is there is a limited supply. Houses burn, get struck by meteors, or exist in declining neighborhoods, which drives up the prices for the choice homes even higher.

More and more, families are being forced into manufactured housing in communities where they will never own the land beneath them. Now, let me make it perfectly clear, there is absolutely nothing *wrong* with manufactured housing except a lot of negative connotation. Several hurricanes have proven that such structures, when properly anchored, are surviving these storms better than site-built, stick homes. If you haven't looked at manufactured housing recently, you are in for a tremendous surprise!

Many are high quality and are cost efficiently built indoors, away from the elements. In response to the demand, there is a growing industry providing communities for these homes that are up to at least middle class or higher standards. I know of several where prospective residents have driven through, admired the models and not even realized there were in a 'trailer park.' I have myself driven through one where it is more common to see luxury automobiles parked outside the attached garages than aging pickup trucks. Times are changing but this may only be a temporary 'dry spot' if trends continue. The second class dining room may be dry and warm with the flooding contained to the lower decks… but chances are it will not last. And when this last timber in the foundation finally rots through, when a significant percentage of the population can no longer keep a roof over their own heads, there will be problems… there will be *significant* problems!

If you take anything at all away from this section, think of this: Income Disparity… it's at the very root of such problems as; the decline of the American Family, the divorce rate, the crime rate, the failures of our education system, the ever-expanding Welfare/Medicaid roles, an increasing foreign presence in our marketplace, the housing shortage, and the housing surplus (the shortage of affordable homes and the surplus of overpriced ones. Just listen to builders talk sometime!). So, Income Disparity, it really is a *thing!*

An Unresponsive Government: This is no surprise. How can you have a discussion about what's wrong with America, and *not* include the

Government? The surprise to some will be that Income Disparity beat it out for the number one spot on the list. But think about it. If the problem with Government is that it doesn't respond to your needs, in fact, doesn't respond at all... not even to return your phone calls, it may be a problem. A big one, even. But *not* as big as your weekly paystub. But not to worry. While we will address some of the issues here, the Government will get their time in the spotlight in Part Two!

Some people say "The road to Washington is paved with broken promises." So often that seems to be true, but why? Why do the new candidates (be they young or old) come around to your doorstep to court your vote, but when they get elected, it's like they disappeared from the face of the earth? You're lucky to hear anything from them at all and then, it's usually in a form letter/e-mail that generically covers all issues and doesn't commit to much of anything... let alone the more urgent issue that motivated you to reach out to them in the first place. Why does that happen?

It happens because we pretty much have only two political parties, both of whom are more concerned with the power struggle between themselves than they are with you and the struggles in your life. Fact.

Every election, we send what we hope are concerned citizens from our local community to be our representatives in Washington. (Actually, this whole section also holds true for our state capitols as well.) Once they leave us and step over that line called the Washington Beltway... they disappear. Gone forever. We never seem to hear from them again and if we do, they no longer seem to be the people we voted for. It's as if some 'Stepford' process has replaced them with an exact clone. What happened? Two things happened.

First, whichever of those two parties our concerned citizens thought they were affiliated with when they decided to run for office; that same party they registered with and shared the ballot with on Election Day; *that* party... they kidnapped them! Pure and simple.

As soon as you walk in the door as a grinning Congressional newbie, you are strong-armed by your respective party's 'Whip,' which is a *real* position by the way and yes, this is their job. You are told where to toe the line in this big picture called "D.C." and you quickly learn that with your election, you have moved up a level and are now desperately needed to represent the party's views on the floor of the House or Senate. You are now a soldier in *their* army. Unless you support the party properly, that same party that decides which committee assignments you get and where legislation sits on the agenda calendar, your ideas, the promises you made to us back home… well, they're just not going to happen.

They desperately need you and your vote on the floor to wrestle power away from that *other* political party that is right now telling their own new people the exact same thing. Assurances are made that if you play along, 'fight for the greater good,' there will be a time and place for your ideas 'once the war with the bad guys is won.' Of course it never is. And if you don't play ball in this power game, you will get your butt sent off to the committee that counts pencils and allocates facial tissues until the next election when they can replace you with someone else.

This is the *party* telling you this, as in 'people who weren't elected by anyone.' It's *Management*. But it's all enforced by the long term members of House and Senate who are on your own side of the aisle, convincing you, coercing you into presenting a united front in order to pull power away from the other team. Think of it like going to a prison where the longer serving inmates actually get to be the guards! That's the first thing that happens to the people we vote for.

But hang on to your hats for the second thing! While it sounds a lot nicer and a lot less dark, it is truly more evil than the first thing and will explain all the other questions you have remaining on this topic: *Money*. It's money, pure and simple. Money, position, power… and yes, that all starts with money!

I know it sounds like we pay Representatives and Senators a lot (currently about $174,000 a year plus benefits. Majority/Minority leaders, etc. make a little more). Compared to many of us, that *is* a lot but is usually countered with arguments about how they have to maintain two households (one back home in their district by law, and one in *very* expensive Washington). If they are younger and take their kids to D.C. with them, well, the *better* people send their kids to a selection of private schools. It's all justified by saying: "Well think of the security issues if the children of Congress went to *Public* School!"

So it's expensive. And even with those big salaries, there's not a lot left over at the end of the day… we are told. Yet, so very many of our representatives who left middle or upper-middle class incomes with modest personal wealth to go to Washington, later leave this public service as multi-millionaires. How does this happen? That's a good question and with all the investigating that seems to be going on up there these days, this is something *I* would personally like investigated. But I truly doubt that will ever happen. (Do you really think they will vote to investigate themselves?)

We get told it was some wise investing, a successful book deal we heard nothing about, and probably some speaking fees as well. But the truth is, there is a lot of money floating around Washington in the pockets of corporate campaign donors, lobbyists, special interests groups, and even the political parties themselves. As much as they deny it, there are ways of 'laundering' such funds through legitimate campaigns, initiatives, and charitable action groups to actually benefit those struggling on that $174,000 a year. (A lot of vengeful promises will be made when someone reads that! But again, this is all my personal opinion.)

The problem is, once someone is elected to this lofty office, they become (willingly or not) part of an 'elite class' in Washington Society. It is a belief, an attitude, perpetuated by those who have been there too long, and by the party who uses this 'old boys and girls club' to bring you into the fold. There are functions and cocktail parties that are important to attend because… that's where business is *done!* And this is *how* it's done. But remember, someone else is paying for it all. And while you are there, conducting business, you will meet those who represent special interests, the big party donors, and the more powerful members of your new club. You will become well-versed on who and what and when and where with whom, and the stance you should take on this or that and the other thing. Notice, there was no 'why' on that list.

The bottom line is, you become completely embroiled in *their* issues and what *they* feel is important, as you become more and more distant from the old folks back home and the reason you decided to run for office in the first place. If you're a Senator, six years goes by pretty quick. And if you're a Member of the House, it's three times quicker. Soon, it's time for re-election and it seems like you're still just getting your feet wet. But do you really have to worry about re-election?

If the party likes you (because you're a stand up guy/gal and did what you were told, even taking the lead here and there), you probably don't have to worry too much. They will line up corporate donations and help set up the super pacs for those nasty attack ads you'll need, and if that's not enough, the party will dump tons of money into your race they collected at $15,000 a plate dinners from the other side of the country. They'll bury your opponent for you, so that you can continue fighting the 'good fight' right there in either the blue or red chairs. If it's near census time, the party may even help you 'adjust' the boundaries of your district to your advantage to help keep you in office, to help keep you in the fold for as long as you can breathe. By this time, you may even have trouble remembering where 'home' is. It's probably not as nice as the one your Washington friends helped you get after the last election, but you'll go back when necessary to take a bow, shake hands with the right people and get your smiling face on the news.

And all because... that's the way it's done. If you're lucky, some small piece of legislation you wrote in your first term might get tacked on to the apron strings of another more important bill just to placate you, and maybe it will even get passed and signed by whatever president is there by then. But relax. You're employed, you're living well, you've got great healthcare and other benefits and you know what else? If Congress is in session, they can't even arrest you for a crime! True! Because someone might use that to keep you from voting on the floor, so it's a law. You're also safer than those back home because you have special laws to protect you, too. If someone takes a notion to shoot you, there are stiffer penalties for murdering members of our ruling class... like Congressmen, Senators, Presidents, or Judges. If one of your constituents gets murdered, they're just dead.

So to answer the question I posed at the start of this section, 'why is our government so unresponsive to the needs of the people? Why don't they listen to us?' The answer is quite simple. All the power in Washington is controlled by two parties, each with their own agenda and set of special interests. They've got the power because they have the money. We as mere voters can't afford to *buy* the attention of the ruling class. We can't *afford* to talk to them, not like the big donors and the party can. Not like the lobbyists can. We are their 'inconvenient truth' they must deal with every election cycle and other than that, we are little more. And why is that? Because the two party system has evolved into such a 'hate-fest,' such a struggle for control, such a pitch battle, there is no time for anything else. To watch it all with an unbiased eye from the safety of a thousand miles away, it all looks like the biggest pie-fight ever filmed by the Three Stooges.

[18]

And all this leads to our next problem:

Partisan Hate: I'm officially a senior citizen. But in my defense, that means I've seen a number of presidents, congresses and captivating political issues come and go over the decades. One thing you could always bet on, Republicans and Democrats have never gotten along. However, what we considered bold and brash behavior just forty years ago, somehow became the norm about thirty years ago. And the bad behavior of *that* era, would later become the 'norm' we longed for just ten years after that. I can safely say, and I'm sure I'll have lots of agreement on this one, I have *never* seen the two major political parties, *this* divided, *this* polarized, *this* filled with hate for each other than I see today. The only other time I can think of that comes close to comparison, is the time leading up to the Civil War.

There was a time when there was hope for compromise somewhere in the middle of every issue. In fact, that was the way things got done! There was frank discussion, man to man (and yes, women, too) in the same room where often, the media was not present. Deals were cut, compromises made and legislation got passed. The country's business got done and things moved forward. Remember those days?

Today, both parties seem incapable of passing anything unless they have an unquestioned majority in Congress with strong-armed Party Whips to keep all their peeps in line. And as soon as one party doesn't get their way, they are off to tell the media how insensitive and uncompromising the opposition is. They whitewash each other with broad brushes with statements like, "All Republicans feel this way" or "All Democrats want that." The world is *never* that black or white. But to listen to them, the end of the world is coming and it's all the fault of the other team. Of course, this will start a domino effect of disaster if our party doesn't stand together, and tell the media, who will then whip up public opinion... and so on. Every issue becomes a sit-down strike and when it's all said and done, darn little actually gets accomplished.

If this weren't bad enough on its own, every time someone suggests compromise, or that the distance between the two positions is not insurmountable, both sides will gasp at the indignity and redefine their position by taking yet another half step toward the extreme ends of the political spectrum. Every issue causes the party whips to line up the troops in

[19]

support while the party leaders carefully… yet defiantly, stand before the microphones and spin fiction into fact about the other side and all their lies.

Now, the problem with *that*, is over time, it has pushed both parties to the opposite extremes of the scale to where neither one *truly* communicates with the public. While an alleged 47% tend to always vote Democrat and yet another 47% tend to always vote Republican, I truly believe that if given a legitimate third choice in the middle, both ends would crash and burn. The majority of Americans just don't agree with the entire platform of either party anymore. I remember a conversation with an old friend of mine at a pool party sometime back. The topic was how you can't play nice with the Democrats unless you accept their most extreme views on gun control, and you can't get along with the Republicans unless you pledge support to Right to Life. I was asked where I felt the majority of Americans stood on the spectrum. I remember telling him that I felt they wanted the 'right to chose' and would want their guns to defend it. Everyone laughed… then, everyone agreed.

To put it graphically, I think the two sides are so far apart from each other, neither one can see the other end of the spectrum anymore. What they *think* they see, is really just that large bump in the middle that is the vast majority of us. It's like climbing a large hill and then you find out what you thought was the top, was only the halfway point.

To wrap this part up, it has never ceased to amaze me how old friends who used to sit down and casually discuss things face-to-face without a complete meltdown, now post hateful, partisan bullshit on Facebook… just echoing the hate they are told from the extreme members of their preferred end of the spectrum. Yes, there is partisan hate out there, it starts at the top of the two parties and is whipped to a fervor before being spoon fed to the rank and file on Capitol Hill. If we want it to end, we need to stop calling people the "Great Cheeto" or "that Witch with the broom." That's schoolyard bully stuff and only adds to the great division we suffer today. (Nobody, NOBODY gets to say, "but he said it first!") The way things are now done, this hate all bleeds over into the media who *somehow* became willing participants in all this. And the media feeds it all back to us in the name of ratings…

Do you think your News Coverage might be Biased? If you don't think so, you really need to start watching more than one channel, or reading

[20]

more than one newspaper or magazine. The more news sources you tap into, even some that are off-shore, you'll start to realize there are more than two sides to every story. Sometimes, there are three, four, or more. When you start to notice that certain sources omit 'facts' the other source led with, and that you are angered by one but not the other, when the same story sounds like two different events according to two different sources... you have to know *someone* is shaping this content to fit an agenda and every agenda serves someone's purpose... and it's usually not yours.

The agenda may be only the chief news editor's own personal political leanings. This is wrong in my book, but you see that these days. Then why is he/she the editor? Because of ratings. Presenting the news as opinion rather than just boring facts gets people fired-up and on the edge of their seats. It keeps them tuned in for more of the 'outrageous' goings on. (Outrage is a terribly overused word these days, don't you think?) And at least with 47% of the market's viewership, it will hit home and ratings have always equaled advertising revenue.

I told you, I am old school and I remember the days when TV newscasters had the word "Editorial" superimposed at the bottom of the screen whenever they were expressing opinion over fact. Newspapers even had a special section called "Editorial" that was contained away from the front page.

These were the days of The Huntley and Brinkley Report, Harry Reasoner, John Chancellor, and of course, Walter Cronkite. They presented facts, both sides of the story and let the viewers make up their own minds. They brought us speeches, not edited sound bites, and showed us unedited images of what really happened, no matter how disturbing. The news was the news as were the newspapers. In fact, you weren't even considered a newspaper unless the word 'integrity' had been bestowed on you by some reputable source and never allowed to tarnish. Bias wasn't even in their vocabulary. And to paraphrase Cronkite, "That's the way it was." (Now remember, this entire book, and especially this following section, is comprised of my own *personal opinions* which I am entitled to express, and to publish under the rights given me by the 1st Amendment to the Constitution.)

Compare that to today. The 'News' has become a 'Show' and thinly veils their political orientations. Some are only one step above a political advertisement. Want what my personal opinion considers specifics?

I had watched NBC's Today Show every weekday morning for well over fifty years. In that time, I saw some of the true greats in broadcast journalism come, and go. Did you know, do you remember, they used to have a 'News Desk?' Right there as part of the set. Every morning, the hosts would greet you, perhaps mention a headline, and then turn the show over to the behind-the-desk newscaster who would give us all the details in the tradition of those mentioned above.

But in more recent years, the show changed. Over time, the hosts greeted you with more than just a headline and time at the News Desk was slowly reduced. Eventually, the News Desk was eliminated completely. Ann Curry, who was the last to sit there, was moved to one of the hosts' chairs and the 'news' was then handled from the Main Desk, and often commented on by other hosts as it was shared with the public. Reporting the News became discussing the News... just in case we didn't know what opinion to make of it all.

Then, things changed suddenly, and even more dramatically. One day, Ann Curry was gone and replaced by the bubbly, ever effervescent (my opinion) Savannah Guthrie with the tall, toothy, brilliantly white smile. She didn't seem to have the experience or the credentials of her predecessors, but it seemed the producers were now looking to ratings. At that moment, it was apparent to me the NBC Today Show had shifted from being a morning news program to strictly a morning talk show.

And also in my opinion, Savannah's personal political leanings were completely transparent. She was absolutely liberal, and all about 'girl power' and anything about the rising feminine. I remember once watching her dance to Gloria Gaynor's "I will survive," on air, with a defiantly raised fist while leading all the other women on the set that day. It was quite a group shot.

These were also the months leading up the 2016 election cycle. It was completely obvious to me that she was a devout Democrat, and a big fan of Hillary Clinton who was then looking forward to being the 'first woman president of the United States.' And with an equal passion, Savannah seemed to hate all things Donald Trump and couldn't wait to tell the viewers what gaff, misspeak, or moral outrage had come to light about him overnight. She seemed (to me) to burst with glee when reporting these stories, the smile grew whiter, her eyes sparkled with the excitement of a kid about to meet Santa Claus, all while visibly squirming in her seat. For me, it was hard to watch, but at least there did seem to be *some* degree of counter balance on the desk.

Then, just as suddenly, Matt Lauer was gone, the victim of an indiscretion committed several years before, yet curiously just then brought to light. In the void, Savannah *temporarily* moved over to the lead chair and they brought on Hoda Kotb to lend her a hand.

Honestly, I personally found this unsettling and yet another giant step away from anything that resembled news. Only my opinion, but I truly felt Savannah Guthrie did not belong in the lead chair. I felt she was biased, more concerned with issues that didn't pertain to me, but most important, I didn't feel she had done or accomplished anything that gave her the credentials as a newscaster for anything more than fluff-piece journalism. She was certainly no Barbara Walters, no Jane Pauley, no Katie Couric… and no, not an Ann Curry either. And now, she sat in the lead chair of the nation's longest running morning news program. And beside her, a woman who was perhaps most noted for excessive on-air wine drinking before noon.

I felt it was imbalanced and a shift in emphasis I did not like. And on the day they announced the change was *permanent*, I changed the channel. After fifty plus years, I changed the channel and I have never gone back.

But where did I go? I looked at the competition. CBS's morning show was going through their own sudden changes with Charlie Rose also getting caught in the '#metoo' purge. And I was no fan of Fox or their tendencies to lean the other way. So this left ABC and Good Morning America. At least their news desk seemed stable and relatively balanced. But they, too, are not without their journalistic problems.

Her name is Cecilia Vega and again, this is all my own opinion. She is the senior White House correspondent for ABC and please note, I did *not* use the word journalist connected to her name. On more than one occasion, I have seen her start her report with "President Trump told another lie overnight when he said…" She hasn't even told us what he said yet, and she has already labeled it a lie? And then she immediately follows this single sentence lead-in with, "The *truth* is…" and the paragraph or so that supports her single sentence opening statement.

[23]

I have never in my life seen a newscaster, so bold, so arrogant, as to tell me what's a lie and what's the truth... especially before she even says what that alleged lie or truth is. Every time she does this, the likes of Walter Cronkite and Edward R. Murrow turn over in their graves... Again, only my opinion. I don't have live camera feeds of either grave.

I know I have spent a lot of time on these two, but only to make my point. There are others, of course, *many* others. NBC's Chuck Todd pops to mind first. While he has made many partisan statements (in my opinion) over the years, nothing seemed to bother me as much as his performance during the 2012 election returns. Most times he referred to the Republican candidate, he simply called him 'Romney' yet, when making similar references to Obama, it was most always 'Our President.' In fact, I can clearly remember the moment when NBC declared the election for Obama, it was 'Ladies and Gentlemen, our president has been re-elected.' Gee, what side do you think he was pulling for?

You don't often hear such adoration in a newscaster's voice but it made me think of the days of shortwave listening and the booming signals on the air from the old Soviet Union talking about their own 'glorious leaders.' Or the brief translations we get of broadcast news clips from North Korea. In those days, I remember thinking I'm so glad we live in a free country with a free press, free of such propaganda. And now these days, I wonder... And like I said, there are *many* other examples I'm certain you are now thinking about as well. (Can you feel the warmth of all those books burning yet?)

But it's not just the newscasters that pose a problem with our media. (Note: I did not say, 'news.') It's the editors, directors and executives as well. Trying to give them the benefit of the doubt, their motivations could be many. It could be for they consider 'the greater good,' or to right a previous injustice, or even just selfish political preferences. But whatever the reason, it's still 'shaping' the news to fit an agenda not yet shared by the viewer. That, in its broadest definition, is propaganda.

Let me site two quick examples, separated by years, and covering different topics. First, let's go back to that 2016 election cycle and again, let's pick on NBC's Today show. I live in the Eastern Time Zone so we catch both hours of that broadcast live. They are tape delayed for other sections of the country. It was about a week before the election. Just at the end of the first hour, the hosts and a guest were discussing the tightening gap in the polls between Clinton and Trump. Just before commercial break, one said, "There's even one poll out this morning that shows Trump in the lead." There were shocked looks all around followed by the usual, we'll be back after this break.

My wife and I heard/saw that live moment together and were also shocked. When I got to my computer, I searched various presidential polls and yes! There was indeed one, published just that morning that put Trump in the narrowest of leads. Again, it doesn't matter *who* you supported during this volatile time in our history, the story here is *how* it was handled by the media!

Throughout the course of the day, I had occasion to discuss this surprising factoid with other friends and family via phone, e-mail and social media across the country. But when this conversation reached a family member in California (a very vocal Clinton supporter), he exploded, denied it, said it didn't happen. He even said he had watched the first hour of the Today Show himself (on time delay) and knew the report but had heard no such reference to the new poll. There was a predictable argument where he said, he'd gone back to the network's web page and replayed the broadcast. At his insistence, so did I. And he was right! In the archived version of this broadcast for the public to stream at their convenience, the same version that aired to those in western time zones, that last line before the commercial break was *missing!* I showed my wife, she couldn't believe it. She had seen it as well… but here it was, *gone!* Someone had edited the tape replay to eliminate that comment! Over half the country never got the chance to hear it. You have to ask yourselves, why?

So, what difference does it/did it make? Well, off the top of my head, this may not have been the only such incidence of this type of tampering with the truth. (And truly, that's what it is.) And if the truth was tampered with by several popular media outlets, it would lead to a false perception of reality. It could… lead a large number of people who all live west of the Mississippi river, to feel their candidate's election was in the bag as they never received the information that the race was tightening into the 'too close to call' territory. It could lead them to be completely caught off guard at the outcome and since this turn of events came out of the proverbial blue, it may have caused some to think the election was stolen or defrauded in some manner. It could lead individuals to protest in the streets by smashing windows and burning automobiles. It could have led to serious injury or death of innocent people. Such violence is disturbing even when it's over the truth… but to find out a media altered perception was at the bottom of it all, still today, tends to be 'unbelievable.'

Here's another example that will open old wounds and create a lot of fights because it's such a polarizing topic. Let's look at how the media handled the Trayvon Martin case some years back. Now, let me emphasize, it does *not* matter here whether you felt Trayvon was senselessly murdered, or that George Zimmerman did so in self defense. This is about how the *Media* handled it.

When this case first erupted in the news, the picture we were continually shown to identify Trayvon Martin was several years old. It showed a brightly smiling young boy of about thirteen, even though there were more recent photos available of a slightly more sinister looking (my opinion) seventeen-year-old in a hoodie, smoking and flashing hand signs to the camera. We saw the old photo a lot! To this day, when you think of Trayvon Martin, when you Google Trayvon Martin, you are presented with this same, more favorable image of an innocent young boy just entering his teen years. Realize it or not, agree with it or not, it does indeed affect your perception of the entire incident.

Now, let's talk about images of George Zimmerman. The most memorable images of him are those from the security cameras in the police station when he was first arrested. This footage surfaced just a couple of days after the incident when we were all too busy taking sides, forming arguments and closing ranks to notice a subtle piece of editing.

Now, remember, the news had been choked with bits and pieces of the event, out of which a nation was still trying to make sense. Zimmerman had claimed Martin had confronted him, started an argument and punched him in the nose. When Zimmerman collapsed to the sidewalk, Martin allegedly climbed on top and started bashing the back of Zimmerman's head into the concrete. According to Zimmerman, just before he would have lost consciousness, he managed to pull his gun from its holster and shot, killing Martin. That's Zimmerman's explanation of the events. Later, ballistics did confirm Zimmerman's bullet traveled upward through Martin's body, killing him.

That's when the surveillance video from the police station surfaced. I first saw this footage a little after seven AM Eastern Time that morning. It was black and white, foggy, but you could indeed see a hand-cuffed George Zimmerman climbing out of the back of a squad car in a police garage. As other officers moved about, one, the one who had helped him out of the car, stopped him in full foggy view of the camera and could be seen examining the back of Zimmerman's head. He touched a certain spot gingerly and repeatedly, looking at it intently from a couple different angles before leading him up the stairs and into the station.

To some, it looked like the officer was examining a wound on the back of Zimmerman's head, which would have supported that version of events. But in all the footage, there was no stream of blood flowing from the wound and even though Zimmerman had extremely short and thinning hair, the lower resolution of the cameras showed no obvious visible sign of an open cut. Those first to demand justice for Trayvon, pointed to this as proof, Martin had never touched Zimmerman who had simply murdered him in the street.

I watched this footage air on national television as my wife and I got ready for work. I said to myself at the time, "Well, that looks convincing." When my wife came back into the bedroom some twenty minutes later, I told her about the footage and when the story started to cycle (repeat) again, I told her to watch, right…

But that few seconds of the video, just the part where the officer examines the back of Zimmerman's head… was gone! He was shown climbing out of the squad car in cuffs, takes a moment to stand up straight and then 'click' he's crossing the garage floor from a different camera angle and then, there was an edit back to the original camera angle, where we see the footage of him climbing up the stairs or ramp into the station. In that length of time, just twenty minutes on the fly, someone had somehow, for some reason, edited that footage! Who would do that, that wasn't trying to influence your perception of the incident?

Like I said, those demanding 'justice' pointed to this altered footage as proof Zimmerman was lying about the attack. They asked, 'but where's the blood, then?' even though ambulance drivers at the scene had stated they had treated Zimmerman and cleaned up his wounds.

[27]

If you Google these incidents today, you will indeed see the full footage complete with the officer inspecting the back of Zimmerman's head. You will also find, high resolution photos, in full color, of Zimmerman's busted nose and the bleeding wound on the back of his head taken at the scene. Those who were against Zimmerman screamed the photos had been faked, that it wasn't even Zimmerman, and quickly those photos disappeared from the media. We wouldn't see them again until they were entered as evidence at his trial. Personally, I find it hard to believe a 'fake photo off the Internet' could be allowed as evidence. When you Google those images, you will find they were published by the Telegraph Newspaper (London), the BBC and Reuters news services. But again, let me emphasize, this is *not* about whom you feel personally was in the right or wrong. This is now about your *perception* of events. *This* is about how the *Media* directed the story.

So very many people were amazed and shocked when Zimmerman was acquitted, not believing justice could be so perverted. Do you think it's possible you were surprised by the outcome because you didn't have all the information the Jury had? What followed was predictable. Florida's infamous 'Stand Your Ground Law' was blamed (which has a catchy name, but really not too different from any other self defense law found throughout much of the country), that blame was transferred then to the gun itself and that led to protests against the NRA and calls for gun bans nationwide. But do you think that *maybe* those opinions, those actions, were formed by edited footage, missing photos and biased news reports? Do you think there is a possibility the Media itself 'helped' this story unfold in this direction and then focused attention along someone else's agenda?

I was going to close this section out with just two examples in the interest of 'getting on with the story.' But as I was writing this passage, another glaring example of a biased media caught the headlines. This was written in the days surrounding the Boeing 737 Max airplane crashes in Africa and Indonesia. The similarity between the two crashes in this new aircraft raised questions of a possible software glitch in the automated systems. Around the world, over the course of just a few days, the entire fleet was grounded by country after country until these issues could be examined. Everywhere, *except* in the United States! Despite cries from the public to ground the planes, Boeing insisted they were safe and they continued to fly.

[28]

Then one morning, I saw on the news where Trump had just signed a Presidential Order grounding all the 737 Max aircraft. He said something about he had signed it and ordered the FAA to carry it out. By early afternoon that day, most news sources were reporting the grounding and by evening news-time, they were all on the ground. But the story I had followed all day, seemed to take a strange twist when it hit the networks. All the American media sources were reporting that the FAA had grounded the planes as if it were the FAA's idea. One source never mentioned Trump at all, another said something about the grounding was 'clarified' later by an order from Trump but none gave him any credit for this action what so ever.

Now, personally, I am no big fan of Donald Trump. Really, I am not. But I *am* a big fan of the *truth*, no matter how ugly or uncomfortable it may be. It was a straight forward chain of events: Trump, Executive Order, carried out by FAA, all planes grounded. Period. Does the American media hate him *that* much that they would minimalize, or even completely remove his involvement in this event, and then misrepresent that same chain of events to us, the American public? We all have to ask ourselves two questions: 1; Why? And, 2; Where else have they done this?

These are only three examples. There are so very many more, all you have to do is leave your loyalties (to the left or the right) on the curb and just watch and listen to what they present to you. Go to multiple sources. Raise questions yourself and then draw your own conclusions about whether or not our media today is biased. Point of information here: There is a streaming news service that recently began operation whose slogan is: 'Be informed, not influenced.' So obviously, I'm not the only one who thinks this is an issue.

I would like to welcome back to this chapter, all of you who have recently burned your copy of this book, but then repurchased once you started to hear about the crazy things I will be discussing in Part Two. I thank you and again, as a retiree living on Social Security somewhere in a trailer park in Michigan, I really do appreciate your added royalties. But before we go on to the fun stuff where the book burners may cheer and the other side may start seeking their lighters, wait. I'm not quite done insulting the Media yet.

I can't tell you exactly when or where it began, but over the last thirty years or so, I've witnessed our news going 'soft.' And by that I mean, slowly, over time, we have been shielded from strong language, offensive images,

[29]

violence, and anything else that might cause you to turn away. It often comes with words from the anchors that tell us 'this footage is just too hard to watch," or some such excuse before they show us blurred images, freeze framed footage, or a video that suddenly 'ends' just before the event that makes it newsworthy. Someone has seen it, heard it, and determined *for* us that we should not. That's what I mean when I say the news has gone 'soft.' Just today, I saw a morning news show promotion on TV that featured the two smiling anchors. He said: "We'll give you the hard-hitting news and facts you need to start your day." (Though, I have personally come to doubt that). And then She says: "And the uplifting stories you need to start your morning on a high note." That says a lot right there and tends to point a finger as to when it happened.

As more and more women joined the workforce and started to share that same morning news/evening news schedule with the men, many objected to the content and the "news" was re-shaped to attract a changing demographic. At the same time, the 'face' of the on-screen news also evolved to present a more pleasing appearance. Face it, Walter Cronkite and Chet Huntley were never going to make the cover of GQ! But these days, it's more important to look 'marvelous' than to speak the truth.

And for some strange reason, we all went along with it. Perhaps it was some chemical in the polish we used on all those participation trophies, or maybe the endorphins left over from that last 'feel good' feature story. Whatever the reason, it happened and having seen the change, both the before and after, it is my opinion we should not have done this.

Understand, I came of age during the 1960s. I saw the Abraham Zapruder film, in its entirety, on broadcast television… again and again and again. We all questioned the direction Kennedy's head jerked after the third shot and then analyzed the Warren Commission report later. I saw Oswald shot on live TV, again, with all the replays in case you questioned how easily Jack Ruby got through the barrier. I also saw Bobby Kennedy and George Wallace shot while campaigning. There were others. I also saw the Vietnam War rage during the dinner hour complete with unedited color footage… every night. I also saw the close-up footage of a Saigon Police captain executing a captured Viet Kong infiltrator with a small pistol, and I saw small children running naked down a road, burned by Napalm. All were graphic, hard images to watch. In those days, there was no censoring, no editing, no blurred screens or freeze frame before the crucial moment. There was no good looking newscaster telling us: "We can't play the tape for you because it is just too hard, too vile to air but take our word for it, it was horrific and nasty."

In reality, the news is often hard but something we often *need* to see. I will remind you of Mathew Brady's pictures of the Civil War which brought the horrors and the reality home to the public for the voters to deal with. The same is true of the trenches of World War One and who can forget the iconic photos of World War Two? Mussolini, dead, and hanging by his feet in the town square for all to see. Those people of that time needed to see that the page of history had turned. Just as those that screamed out to question if Hitler had really died because they never saw the proof. We had proof of Hiroshima and Jonestown, and don't tell me seeing those images didn't affect you and the decisions you still make today. In the Gulf War, we saw Saddam's sons, dead and then later, leaked cell phone footage of his own hanging. It was closure.

But feel the difference a few years makes. When Osama Bin Laden was killed by Seal Team Six, we were not allowed to see pictures of his dead body... They were 'too hard' for us to see and it was feared the images might piss off our enemy even more. Yet, the terrorist who masterminded the greatest mass murder/attack we have ever suffered was buried at sea, with no photos. Burial at sea is also an affront to Muslim culture, so if showing his dead body might outrage the enemy (maybe dishearten a few as well?), burying him at sea was okay? All that did was give fuel to the conspiracy theorists that he is still alive in captivity someplace, never to be seen again. And all because, we never saw the proof.

The truth, reality, can be hard to face and difficult to watch. But we need to do these things. If we insulate ourselves from the harshness of it all, it becomes too easy for us to agree to continue a policy or a war that otherwise we might force to come to an end. We can't sit behind our blurred images and incomplete footage and eat cake while we contribute to things we might later see as injustices. Remember how many German citizens were horrified when they finally got to see the insides of the Concentration Camps. Had they seen this sooner, perhaps Hitler's support would have faded? Perhaps he would have met an earlier end? What about our own Civil Rights movement and the wrenching, iconic images of Black men and women being attacked with fire hoses and police dogs? Would the absence of these images have changed the outcome of that era?

I can tell you, firsthand, those bloody images from the battlefields of Vietnam were a factor that helped bring that war to an end. Over time, it wasn't just the long-haired, 'Anti American Hippie Types' who had had enough. Eventually, Middle America had seen all they wanted to see as well and ending the war became a campaign issue. Yet here we are, in a war that has lasted even longer than Vietnam and I can't help but feel that perhaps our filtered, softened view of the world may be a factor. Blurring an image doesn't make it go away.

If the reality of news footage bothers you, look away. And if reality causes you to look away, maybe we should make efforts to change that reality rather than freeze frame it, chocolate-coat it, and continue on with our happy lives. We shouldn't be watering down the truth to make it palatable to our gentle psyches. It's like Marie Antoinette saying only the more attractive peasants are allowed to lineup outside the palace gates.

The whole situation reminds me of an old episode of the original Star Trek TV show from the mid-60s. In this episode, Kirk and the Enterprise enter a star system where two planets have been at war for over five-hundred years. Early on, both planets decided they wanted to preserve their culture, their art, and their buildings from the destruction of war, so, by treaty, the war was now fought by computers. (Like a computer game a good thirty years ahead of its time!) One computer would attack with virtual missiles and the other planet's computer would defend, back and forth like a giant game of Battleship. Yet another computer registered the success and location of each attack and would calculate casualties. Then, citizens from those areas were informed of the attack and had twenty-four hours to report to a 'disintegration chamber.' Nice, neat, no mess. If either side failed to disintegrate the proper number of casualties, the treaty would be broken and the war would resume with 'live ammunition.'

Long story short, Kirk caused one side to violate the treaty by destroying their disintegration chambers (and saving a pretty girl in the process). When the head of their high council shouts at him, "Do you realize what you have done?" Kirk answers, "Yes, I've given you back the horrors of war." He explains how it's the death, the destruction, the devastation of war that will finally give you the courage and determination to end it. Everyone must see it in order to bring about change. I ask you, by blurring, freeze-framing, or just 'softening' our news, aren't we doing the very same thing?

In closing this section, I want to tell you about the scariest thing I heard during the 2016 election cycle. I found myself in a conversation with a devoutly Democratic Millennial who seemed quite relaxed with his stance and his decisions. I asked him if he'd seen a particular story on the network news the night before.

"Oh, no…" he said dismissing me. "I get all my news from Twitter."

"Twitter?" I said, surprised. "Isn't that where Trump does all his lying?" I baited him. Again he shook his head and dismissed my comment.

"You know, some really trusted news people have their own shows you can only see on Twitter." He went on to name several left wing pendants noted for their anti-right rants.

"Their own shows, like, there's no one there to balance, to raise questions or counter challenge anything they say?"

"They're going to say it anyway. But this way, I can get all the news I need in five or ten minutes."

"But if Trump is allowed to lie on Twitter, how do you know what the *truth* is?"

"Listen," he said, his temper growing short. "It's simple. Everything Trump posts is a lie. Most everything else is true."

"Most?"

"Yeah, most. You've just got to be smart enough to filter out the bullshit."

"And you can do that?" I asked innocently.

"Every day!" he finished with a nod.

I sighed in disappointment but took comfort in knowing my lifespan would be less than his and I would never live to see the world he and Twitter would vote in.

So, is your news biased these days? Does it present an incomplete story of events? I'd say so. If it seems many of these examples tend to lean to the left in their presentation, Please, I am *not* being unfair. I am actually very, very middle of the road and yes, the right will get their time in the hot seat soon enough here. But for this section, remember, most all our national media outlets are located in large cities and metropolitan areas. These areas tend to lean toward the Democratic side, period. It's perfectly logical the news they present might have a similar lean. That's why it's so important for *good* journalists to consciously approach every story from an unbiased position regardless of their own personal feelings. It's just another thing that's wrong with America. And if we want to get things back on track, it's another thing we'll have to fix.

Abuse by Lawyers: In our society today, we have trained far too many lawyers… far more than we will ever need and many more than we will ever want to hear from again. I think we all know someone who, at the end of one career or job, did some soul searching and decided to go back to school… Law School. Some decide to do this right out of college. Others were 'born' to it. Yet for many, it remains a mid-life crisis.

Their reasons are many and there are many more reasons they won't tell you as some may still be discovering them in therapy. Some will insist they did this for 'the little guy' who needed some noble knight willing to take up their banner and fight for their very existence, out of some 'Horton Hears A Who Complex.' They often justify their self image in shining armor with hopes of being preserved in statuary on hallowed ground someday… like Lincoln. Yet others secretly relish the power of brilliantly arguing a case in court and forcing other people to comply with their way of thought… and emptying their checkbooks in the process. Like I said, the reasons are many and varied. But whatever the reason, we have far too many and so very many of those lawyers end up struggling for their *own* existence, 'looking' for lawyer work that *they* feel needs to be done.

I ask you, who else could turn a minor slip and fall into a multi-million dollar award and if they're lucky, even be the reason for some of the most ridiculous consumer warnings ever published? Notice an increase these past few years in class action suits? You get those notices in the mail and a chance to join in on their 'lottery pool.' I have friends who fill out every one of these things that come in and sure enough, they'll get a check for thirty dollars and change here, or twenty-some dollars there, and it's nice pocket money. But who has put all these cases together? Unemployed lawyers who were looking for something to bill their hours against, that's who. I've had several lawyers tell me, the only people who really make money off of class actions suits, are the lawyers themselves.

[34]

And what is the cost of all this? Well, with all these settlements, you know the cost of everything from fast food coffee to lawnmowers built between this date and that date, and the price of chicken processing... everything... the cost goes up to cover these monumental damage awards. But that's just the financial cost, the social cost has been far worse.

For the most part, well, a major part, I feel the out-of-control level of 'Political Correctness' we suffer with today found its start with a crusading lawyer. And then everyone got involved to the point now where you can't say or do much of anything without raising ire from some faction or splinter group, or risk getting sued yourself. It seems everyone has a voice, a loud voice, even if they have nothing to say. (Just look at me, writing this book! See?)

Everyone wants their own victory in some small sector of the society so at least there, the world revolves around them. Everyone wants to feel empowered because they feel completely disenfranchised in the rest of their lives. And of course, there's always that big settlement check when you win... and that's better than hitting the lottery!

It has created a world where everything has to be somebody's fault... but never your own. There is no such thing as an accident anymore. There is only blame and liability. Not only are we not responsible for our *own* actions, the actions of others are always financially recoverable in a court of 'law.'

I think a lot of that started with young self-righteous lawyers who found their way into the Prosecutor's office or social services departments. That's when we noticed the uptick of poor urban parents being tried for child abuse or neglect whenever a toddler managed to escape a screen door latch. It spread from there up the income scales, though not as prevalent as it is in the lower brackets.

I watched this progress from the state *requiring* you to properly restrain your child in a car, then it was car seats, and then we extended that to booster seats. If you were in an accident and your child died because you didn't keep them properly restrained, you could be ticketed, then later arrested, and then we even started sending them to prison. This quickly spread to your failure to keep cupboard doors latched, car keys out of reach, hot water faucets tightly closed, medications out of sight and guns locked up. I remember when the pain of losing your child out of your own stupidity and the public humiliation that went with all that was punishment enough. But now you can be put

[35]

behind bars by people defending your own dead children, who weren't properly cared for according to someone else's level of expectation. Harsh... but think about it. It can be hard to live up to a crusading lawyer's standards and now, we have been at this so long, it's become the norm.

This problem got more and more out of hand as we became a nation of 'scoff laws,' meaning you can break any minor laws you want because effectively there is no enforcement. "Everyone else does it" so why not you... and your kid? People now run stop signs, speed, give their children age-inappropriate toys and then wonder why things go wrong. Why? Because there is just no enforcement anymore. And each and every one of us gets reminded of this each and every day. Want an example?

Remember the "Do Not Call List" to stop unwanted telephone solicitation? You can register for this and read the laws restricting telemarketers at www.donotcall.gov. However, you'll soon realize it makes no difference. You still get recorded calls and calls from companies you have not done business with in the last 18 months (or ever, even). All these calls are supposedly illegal and the telemarketing companies are supposed to vet their lists against that Do Not Call list before ever dialing you... but they don't. And even when they say they'll put you on their *own* do not call list, they continue to call. If what they are calling about isn't an out and out scam, even if it is a legitimate business or service, the call itself is illegal. But the telemarketing companies don't care because... there is no enforcement of these or many other laws. In fact, they'll call you daily, in the privacy of your own home, just to remind you how powerless you are to stop them. Yup! We are now a nation of Scoff Laws. And this is what parents today are teaching their kids. "Don't worry about it, it's just us and it's just right here. It'll be OK." And then we give that kid a motorbike, or unrestricted Internet access, or a gun...

It has gotten so out of control that even I would agree some of these parents need to be held accountable for their kids' actions, as well as their own. And that's where we crossed the line into the next level of insanity where the best defense became a good offense. Here are a couple examples from my own state of Michigan. I bet you can name a few, too.

In the city of Detroit, some parent gave their underage, teenager a four-wheel ATV to ride around the urban neighborhood. Was this vehicle street legal? No. Was this teen old enough to hold a driver's license? No. Was there a parent supervising how this teen used and abused this unlicensed motor vehicle? No. There is video of this young man doing wheelies and doughnuts in the middle of residential intersections and speeding up and down the streets while much younger children played at the curb.

Michigan State Police rolling through the neighborhood spotted him and tried to pull him over. For whatever reason, out of whatever upbringing, he did not comply and decided to run for it, at high speed, up these crowded, over-parked streets. Did this teenage pose a threat to the community? My opinion only, he absolutely did! Had he run down a small child, the police would be on the hook for not stopping this behavior and enforcing the laws. Had they broken off the chase and let him go, they would still be blamed as he could have killed a child further up the street, or later than same day, or even the next because the situation was allowed to continue.

In a moment of questionable judgment, at a time when a fleeing suspect refused to comply, the State Trooper pulled out his Taser and shot the teen on the ATV. Of course, the teen lost control, hit a parked car and broke his neck. He was dead at the scene but there were no others injured. He posed an active risk to those innocents around him. Had he complied and stopped, he would have been ticketed, his parents called into court and he would have lost his precious ATV he should have never had in the first place. But he'd be alive.

Given what you've already read, you can see where the crusading prosecutor would probably file child neglect charges for this string of poor decisions. But while we were all waiting for that to hit the news, word came they were going to prosecute the State Trooper for causing the teen's death. Charges against the parent never materialized! But in the end, we sent a State Trooper to prison! Yes, he was convicted and sent to *prison*! Where is the logic in this? See, the best defense against those child abuse charges is a good offense, putting all the blame on someone else so people will forget about your own complicity.

It recently happened again in rural Western Michigan where parents had given a ten-year-old what is now called a 'Pocket Bike.' In my youth, we may have called it a 'mini-bike' but it's more motorcycle than mini-bike. In any event, it's an unregistered, motorized vehicle given to an underage operator with zero supervision and allowed to go ride on a multi-lane thoroughfare.

[37]

Now, a Deputy Sherriff, a multi-year veteran of the force, is responding to a call on that same street. He comes up the street without lights and siren as to not worsen the situation he is responding to. When he crowns a hill, he hits this child on his pocket bike, riding down the centerline of the road. The child was killed instantly. Again, no charges for child endangerment, but his family is seen on the news carrying signs outside the courthouse demanding 'justice' for the boy (or, a twenty-five-million dollar cash settlement, whichever comes first). And I sat there wondering why they weren't arrested... after just asking you why we are prosecuting bad parents in the first place. It's confusing times...

One more example that made me wonder aloud: I saw this on the network news but it could have been any urban city in America. A young adult man is high on something, or insane, or both. But for whatever reason, he had got himself a handgun and is walking/trotting through the neighborhood, shooting at things! Cars, houses, even people! But he's so out of it, he's not hitting what he's aiming at. Yet, I supposed at the time, while he might not be aiming at the old lady in her living room, he might have eventually hit one had this been allowed to continue. (It was never made clear, but he seemed to be reloading his handgun from somewhere).

The police were called. A large number of them, on foot, tried to stop this man but he ignored all demands to surrender, to put the gun down, to just stop shooting. He was quick. Just as police thought they had him surrounded to take him down, he'd jump a fence and go up the next street, shooting at whatever caught his attention. Eventually, one of the officers shot the man in the back, killing him. And that's when the 'outrage' started.

People were upset he'd been shot in the back, that police should have just let him go, because after all, he was moving away from them at the time. Does that make sense? If it was my neighborhood, and there was a crazed gunman who had just shot up one street, on the move and on his way to *my* street, I would want the police to stop him, at *any* cost! I say, shoot him in the back if you have to if he won't comply with lawful orders to surrender. This isn't an episode of 'Gunsmoke,' this is my neighborhood where my children play! Yet, there were those demanding murder charges against this police officer who, in my opinion, deserved a medal. The sad part of this is the last I heard, the prosecutor and the department were considering those charges...

[38]

It's a crazy world we have evolved into... we have lost so much 'us', and all the 'progress' we have made in social issues, is to me, of very questionable value. Pull back and look at the 'Big Picture' again with fresh eyes. Because we nitpick, sue, find blame anywhere we can, champion our shortcomings at the expense of the group... Well... because of all that, we have lost our unity in favor of our diversity. We are no longer Americans. We are now defined by the string of adjectives we put in front of that and each and every adjective seems to operate with its own set of rules and privileges.

The problem with all this, is *sometimes*... we *do* get caught, or something else does go wrong, or a tragedy that could not be left as an accident, happens. And then what? And then we call a lawyer who will find a reason, a cause, or a loophole that excludes you and yours from the 'Big Picture.' We will make exceptions to a law, a precedent, a code of ethics and if necessary, we will fight to bend the Constitution to fit our personal agenda. Lawyers tell Judges to put blinders on and ignore that 'Big Picture' and only see this particular event in this exact place and time and then rule on that. But then it becomes a ruling that bends us all. It's no longer about what decision is best for the rest of us, what's best for a culture, a society, a nation moving forward... it's about what exclusions can be made for certain individuals.

This is what I meant when I said we have lost our unity for the sake of our diversity, when we quit seeing ourselves as Americans with anything resembling common goals and values. By now, it's reached a point where you have to say: "Yes, it's broken." Maybe now you can see where it started and maybe you're already thinking of ways to change it. Maybe... you're thinking it's not gone far enough. Maybe you're thinking "Just a little bit further and my own agenda will finally pay off for me." I think you already know what I'm thinking.

So...Have you read enough? How many copies of this book have you burned so far? Are you tired of my tirade of all that's wrong and how nothing is right anymore? Can you see where maybe, just maybe, this is connected to that, and that affected by this? Are you tired of all that, of me? What do you say... we FIX IT! Here are some ideas. Some are mere thought starters, others will seem outlandish, even more may be completely uncalled for unless you are at the wrong end of the stick. So, keep your matches handy.

Part Two
OK, Let's Fix It!

Washington is Broken:

I told you at the top of Part One, that Income Disparity is perhaps the greatest, most singly responsible cause for all our troubles and issues. Fix that, and many of our other problems would *slowly* start to correct themselves. I still stand by this.

But when it comes to actually making changes to *fix* those issues, it all begins with a very broken Washington D.C. (and their subsequent satellites in your own state capitals). And, of the very, very many problems in Washington, number one on the list, without a doubt, is Congressional Term Limits! I'll say it again so that it's perfectly clear. If there is one thing, one change that we could make, one that would over time, tend to heal and correct many of our other ills, if there were only one thing this book might get us to stand up and correct… this is it!

Term Limits: Congress was so kind in the 1940s to put term limits on the office of the President, passed for the most part, by those unhappy with the people's love for FDR. But so conveniently, they forgot to include their own offices in those limitations. We have people, in the House and Senate who have literally been there for decades! I'm going to cite just two examples and a lot of people will hate me for this (maybe even burn this book… again!).

The late John Dingell of Michigan is the first that comes to mind. He held his seat in the House of Representatives for over fifty-nine years! And he won that seat in a special election, succeeding his own father who had held it for over twenty two years before him. In his last years, Dingell decided to 'retire' and endorsed his own, much younger wife as his replacement. And in this heavily Gerrymandered district (go look at maps of the Michigan 12th Congressional District), she has easily won, riding on the political machine built by her husband. (Again, this is all my own personal opinion.) That means, for nearly ninety years, going on a century, a Dingell has controlled

[41]

this seat in the house. That's less like the House of Representatives and more like the House of Lords!

Another I'll take exception to, is the late Senator John McCain. He was in the Senate for over thirty years and wielded much power and influence over others in his party and in the Senate itself. Again, my opinion, but from what I saw on the news feeds, in his latter years, much of McCain's time and effort seemed to be spent on settling personal political battles and grudges than on the needs of the people of Arizona. He had a reputation for having a short fuse and not being afraid of a fight... and it seemed to me he spent too much time doing just those things at the expense of progress. Even when his brain cancer became so advanced he was no longer able to serve in Washington, he went home for medical care and eventually, to die. But he never surrendered his seat in the Senate. He never resigned so the governor could appoint someone to complete his term or at least keep the chair warm until there could be a special election. McCain died a U.S. Senator, leaving the people of Arizona under-represented during his lengthy illness. (Again, my opinion.) But does this sound like it was in the best interests of the people of Arizona, or more about him personally?

I know, there are those who will say both these men did a lot of good things. That's politics, you can't get re-elected if you don't at least keep up appearances. But that much time in office comes with a power and a wealth that grows and builds upon itself. It's an influence the Founding Fathers never intended and can be used and leveraged in ways the electorate may never see or understand. It's too long! It's too much! And you know what? There are lots and lots more of 'those people' out there who have been up there... far too long.

Is too long in office really a bad thing? Many will say that "our representative has been there so long, he knows all the in and outs, he knows how to get things done, he's got seniority over the others and that's good for us!"

Well, you had me right up to the end on that one. They certainly learn quickly how things work and have others showing them how to use that to their advantage. Remember, it's seniority that is used to keep the fresh new faces we send up there toeing the party line. It also keeps their fresh new ideas playing third or fourth fiddle to the needs of the party's agenda. So, while some good may filter down from time to time, the vast majority of that power is used to leverage more power, and more wealth. (Opinion!) The longer any Congressman or Senator is in office, the closer their relationship grows with the special interests and other lobbyists. The longer they are there, the more favors they receive from people we did not elect. And the longer they are there, the more time these special interests have to learn your representative's weak spots... or even their darkest secrets.

Being in Washington too long is not a good thing for the people. It never has been. It only serves to separate your Congressman or Senator from their constituents, and leaves them more likely to find themselves obligated to corporate sponsors and organizations. Too long within the Beltway may also tend to make them feel 'special,' or 'infallible,' and add to the ruling class mentality from which so many seem to suffer. And the longer they are there, the more money they seem to mysteriously acquire.

Think about it. Speaker of the House, Nancy Pelosi, has an estimated worth of fifty-six million dollars. She claims it's really only half that. Still, she has been in the House of Representatives for over thirty years on a salary they all claim to be insufficient. So, how did she acquire such wealth? (I'd like to see *her* tax returns!) From everything I can find, she lives in a mansion in downtown San Francisco surrounded by a security wall. Now remember, she's supposed to represent all the people in that district. But... is the wall around her mansion bigger than the one around yours? What... you don't have a wall around yours at all? And it's not a mansion? I'll ask the obvious: What does she have in common with you to be your peer, your representative? Do you truly believe she is one of your own, representing your needs and best interests? Have you tried to make an appointment to see her lately? Remember, the Sherriff of Nottingham was responsible for the people under his jurisdiction, too. He also collected their taxes and lived behind walls. And FYI, he didn't take appointments, either. But Nancy Pelosi is not alone, only my example. The scary part is, there are lots of Representatives in Washington just like her on both sides of the aisle!

Okay, I hope you can see the general need for term limits now. I truly believe we need to get back to the basics of what the Founding Fathers intended. Service in the House or Senate was never meant to be a lifelong career. It was meant to be a civic duty. One you would perform, and then return to your home and your civilian life while someone else took your place and served their time. A little more like Jury Duty, perhaps. But in the past few generations, it has become widely abused.

What kind of limits should we consider? Personally, I find myself agreeing with many of the polls on this topic. That would be, six terms (twelve years) tops for a member of the House and two terms (again, twelve years) for a Senator. I will also stipulate here, that's twelve years in each chamber of Congress, not twelve years representing that district or state. No district hopping! No, "Well, I've moved here now so I can serve another twelve years representing whoever you people are now." Twelve years is pleanty. This way, if you have someone from your state who is much loved and trusted, he/she could theoretically serve twenty-four years in Washington (twelve in the house, twelve in the Senate), and I would assume, that would be after they had served somewhere in the state structure of government. That still allows them to be a career politician (although unlikely), but not in any one place too long to be uncomfortably close to people not elected by you. Remember: graft is a crop with deep roots that can only grow slowly over time.

One way to force term limits at the grass roots level, is to vote those people out. Right now, they don't need to change because they have a legal, though unethical, grip on the system. Part of their grip on power comes from "stacking the deck" on Election Day. By that, I mean some party campaign manager has run their re-election effort (and attack ads) to assure the candidate who survives to face them will be hopelessly incapable of winning. How many times have we gone into the booth and looked at the ballot only to realize we have a choice between the same incumbent who's been there for years… or a box of rocks.

Given our current situation, our only recourse to eliminating these long-term incumbents is to actually vote for that box of rocks. And by looking at some of the strange people who went to Washington after this last election cycle, that's exactly what some of us did! (Probably planning on replacing them with yet another candidate at the next election.)

While this would be one way to force term limits, it's very inefficient. First, not enough people, in the same election will vote for their respective box of rocks. There would still be enough incumbents re-elected to stack those boxes of rocks that managed to win, safely in the corner. And even if we did somehow find a way to elect enough of those box of rocks candidates to make a difference, would a Congress full of rocks be attuned enough to make the necessary changes? Or would they waste that precious time before the next election making fools of themselves in front of the media?

Now, the sad news: While I hope I have shown you the need for Congressional Term Limits, you need to realize everyone within the Washington Beltway (and in other assorted state capitals) is going to be vehemently opposed to this. It's going to take a Constitutional Amendment to make this happen and the sad news in fact, is that there is no practical way to do this without the approval of the very people you're trying to put out of business. With the exception of only one, all Constitutional Amendments have started in Congress, been approved by both houses before being shipped off to the state capitals for ratification. Even within the provision whereby enough state legislatures (still controlled by the same two parties) demand a Constitutional Convention to introduce an amendment, it *still* falls to Congress to schedule, handle, administer, block, resist or pigeon-hole to death, any such change. Do you really think they wouldn't mind term limits? Do you really think the two parties, who will speak through the most senior members of Congress, do you really think they will let this happen? Either they will say "Sure, let's send it to committee to study it until it dies," or they will simply say "Preposterous! Another Democrat/Republican lie!" And then they will turn their backs again, and resume business as usual…

Now, the shocking news: So, what do we do now? I won't say 'relax,' but the Founding Fathers did provide us a means of resolution for such a situation. It's called the Second Amendment and before those of you who lean to the left go all batty on gun control and anti-violence… think: That's exactly what the majority of those on Capitol Hill and their big financial backers *want* you to do. They don't want a unified people opposing them and they certainly don't want those people to have guns. Their solution so far is to keep us arguing amongst ourselves over this and every other issue.

While we may never agree which Founding Father may or may not have said this, or that, instead of arguing historical semantics, let's look at the big picture here. The Second Amendment was included so that the people of the United States would never be subservient to any government ever again… including their own. Many of you out there have taken the pledge to defend the Constitution from "all enemies, both foreign and domestic." Even Thomas Jefferson said: "The tree of liberty must be refreshed from time to time with the blood of patriots and tyrants." Well, a government that goes to the highest bidder and has lost touch with its people certainly fits the bill of 'tyrannical.'

So what is Jenvey saying? I'm saying there are a lot of people in Washington who have settled themselves into some pretty comfy and cozy situations. Since they are the ones who will have the last word on Term Limits, it's probably not going to happen as long as they are in power. Prediction: They will laugh at you and your demands, and then personally call me treasonous. They will hide behind the Beltway and their party strongmen and say such things as 'the army will suppress any civil disturbance.' They will say 'The police and military are better armed and outnumber any radical band of armed civilians.' And finally, 'The armed forces are sworn to uphold the United States Government.'

Well, let's correct some of that line of thought. Seventy-million gun owners in the United States outnumber our own army several times over. Then consider those seventy-million gun owners are here, in country, while much of our armed forces are scattered around the world. Also consider the fact that many of these seventy-million gun owners (did I get that number in there enough?) were actually trained by that same military. Does the military have better weapons? Yes, but ask anyone who was in the French Resistance about the successful rearmament program they used during Nazi occupation. Here's another thought, the armed forces are actually sworn to defend the *Constitution* and that goes back to that 'all enemies, both foreign and domestic' thing. I truly believe that accepting money from people who cannot vote for you in consideration of favors and at the expense of those who *did* vote for you... are sufficient grounds to label you as 'an enemy of the people.' Besides, every successful revolution usually involves a significant percentage of the military turning around and joining with the revolutionaries. (And those in our current military may have consideration for this after they read my ideas about over-due changes in the armed forces.) Remember, at the onset of the Civil War, over half of our seasoned military leadership, the best of our best, resigned their commissions and joined the Confederacy.

You don't have to think about it as a 'revolution against the United States of America.' We are actually just Americans who want our country back. This would be more of a 'purge' and if you want to go biblical on it all, think of it like Jesus chasing the money lenders from the temple. Although, I don't see Mitch McConnell or Chuck Schumer and their big money friends responding well to being whipped with a palm frond.

Am I advocating armed revolution, right now, against all of Washington? No, I am not. But I want you to be mad enough to do so, *if* need be. I want you to be prepared to pick up your rifles and march on Washington until all those who have been there more than twelve years in either house, pack up and leave. There are those there now who will not take you seriously until you've encircled the Hill and started building a gallows behind the Capital Building. I don't want you to think this is all just silly rhetoric. I want you to understand that the other changes we so *desperately* need, cannot and will not happen unless we get these term limits, *first*. If the Washington ruling class sees the public is dead serious and that corporate donations can't help them here, it could all happen very quietly. But there are those there who may only understand it at the point of a bayonet and the end of a rope. The point is, we need term limits on the members of Congress and you will never get your government back until you get them. No price is too high to pay for that. Okay, scary stuff over. Let's rebuild.

Let's redefine the Congressional Job: With a new Congress full of fresh new ideas and a path cleared of dinosaurs and party bosses, it's now time to redefine the role, the job, and the lifestyle of all Congressmen and Senators.

While they claim it's inadequate, we pay our representatives pretty well. We *could* do it like the Peace Corp did, and each gets paid based on the average income in their home district. Remember, the Peace Corp also required you to live 'with and as,' the people you were helping... not in a nice ranch house on the edge of the village like some plantation owner because that was the standard you were used to, but right there in the huts with the dirty water. But without being silly, I think we can all agree that Congress should not be allowed to vote themselves pay raises and given time, we should be able to come up with some other check and balance system on Congressional pay. I'm not belittling this aspect. It's just that I have so much

[47]

more to follow that will help sort this issue out from the other side. So let's move on.

Part of Congressional compensation has been healthcare and pensions. For many years, members of Congress had the absolute best healthcare our money could buy, and once elected, they got to keep that and their salaries until the day they died, still in office or not.

While many still believe this is the case, I suggest you Google it and see the current facts. Their compensation package has been dialed back some to make it more palatable to the American Public. (I mean, they wouldn't want the people getting pissed enough to take up arms and build a gallows behind the Capital now, right? Don't be ridiculous!) However, it's still extremely generous! They now get a 401K they can roll over when they leave public office that is a lot like yours… except it's far more generous and grows a lot quicker. But this puts the 'nay nay pension sayers' on the defensive and gives Congress the pretense of being humble.

Their health plan is also not what it once was, but they will tell you they have to go to a health care marketplace and buy their coverage just like *you* do! But it's not. They go to a special online marketplace just for members of Congress and buy healthcare coverage you and I can only dream about.

So again, we need to align things. Their compensation is higher than average. (Give me a minute on this one.) But we can certainly bring their retirement packages and healthcare options into line with the rest of us. There is no reason they should not have to buy their health care at *healthcare.gov* like everyone else. Let them live like the rest of us and see how fast things change!

But let's move on to the big banana, the big sticking point that causes a lot of their other problems; housing. You see, Congressmen and Senators have always claimed they needed the pay structure they have enjoyed mostly because they are required to maintain two residences: One in the district or state they represent and another in very expensive Washington.

Every election cycle, there is a major reshuffling of DC real estate. There are the new ones buying in for the first time, those leaving are selling off, and those who stay, are probably looking at moving up. Just like back home, your house and where you live says a lot about you. Unfortunately, the only ones really benefitting from this bi-annual bonanza are the DC area real estate agents! It's an expensive place to live and one that is artificially inflated by

[48]

this regular, predictable wave of turnover. Why are we enriching all these real estate agents indirectly with our tax dollars? (Where did the Congressional paychecks that pay these over-priced mortgages come from? Us!) And this says nothing about the time and effort our representatives spend finding and financing a house, time that could be put to better use serving us.

But I have a solution for this. Now, don't laugh, don't dismiss the whole idea. Chew on this a moment and ask yourself, "why not?" What we need, is government provided, Congressional housing! Think about it! I'm not saying we put them all in some college dorm, but that's the general idea. And for security reasons, you wouldn't want to put them all together in one place. But part of their Congressional compensation would be a free place to live!

This could very well be a series of apartment buildings, condominiums or even ranch-style homes on par with married military officer on-base housing. These would be in gated, secured communities, and all scattered across the D.C. area. It could even be all of these options offering them a (controlled) range of lifestyles! It could very well be *nice* without being *lavish*. There will be those on the Hill right now who will laugh at this but I beg them to remember, they are here to serve their constituents and this would be a nice, secure place to stay, rent free, while here. Also, this would not be an option, this would be required. We don't want any independently wealthy Congressmen opting to buy their own homes on the open market. Just like college freshmen, on-campus living is mandatory. We are redefining the job here. Things will be different than they are now.

In order to get this much housing, completed and on-line as quickly as possible, we may have to resort to manufactured housing. *Wait a minute, did he just say he wants to put all our Congressmen and Senators in a Congressional Trailer Park?* Well… yes… I did! It would be a very *nice* trailer park, a gated community even! Like I said before, manufactured housing today is actually very nice. I live in such a retirement park myself with wide, modern ranches and attached garages. We have people drive through here all the time who never realize they are technically in a 'trailer park.'

About seventeen-hundred square feet or so is all they truly need and there are plenty of homes, just like that in the plants and on dealer lots, right now, ready to go! Think: It would be like putting your kids into school uniforms. No more pushing and shoving on the pecking order to have something nicer than the kid next door. No more worrying about fashion faux pauxs so they can concentrate on their business at hand.

There would be a security savings, too. These would be gated communities (again, not all in one place) where cameras and patrols could be shared rather than each individual representative buying, and then securing their own home at our expense (remember, we are the ones who pay their 'inadequate' salaries). Besides, I have to admit there's something that warms my heart about the thought of the Freshman Congressman from Montana waving at the Speaker of the House across the street as they both take their trash out at the same time.

"But there's no room to entertain!" That's part of the idea. D.C. deals do *not* have to be done at lavish parties! "But that's the way it's done!" It wouldn't be anymore. You can talk politics and compromise just as well over a backyard barbeque as you can at a formal cocktail party paid for by people who did not elect you. Or try this… at work.

Also, we wouldn't want any partisan politics coming into play with their housing, as in *this* is a Democratic neighborhood, or Republican leadership lives *here*. We would want them all mixed in together, regardless of party or rank, so they have a chance to talk, to exchange ideas, even find common ground while riding the elevator in the morning or rolling their trash bin out to the curb with the Speaker. There will be those who say they can't live in this kind of housing, at this level of lifestyle. There's no room for their staff. To that, I would say, tell that to your constituents, first. See how that flies. Then, if it still goes against your grain, perhaps, just perhaps, this job is not for you! Maybe you'd be happier back in the private sector where you can buy any house you want. But while you represent the people of the United States of America, you will live 'on-base.'

And hand-in-hand with where you live, is where your kids go to school. Yes, a good number of representatives come to D.C. with their families. As soon as they find a place to live, they start to search for a private school for the kids. Public School in D.C. might not be the safest, most secure place for a leverageable teenager from Iowa, but private school is going to be expensive on an inadequate salary.

We need to look no further than our own embassies to solve this problem. Children of Diplomats are usually schooled in an 'American

School' right on the premises or in another secured location. Why couldn't we do that in Washington? Think of it, a K-12 Congressional School will keep them safe, secure *and* well-educated! Our expense to do this, *all* this, pales to the amount of money we give away to insurgents and less-than-friendly governments every year. With the savings our new Congress would enjoy with these changes, we might even find it possible to actually *reduce* their compensation? And the savings from that could also go toward offsetting our initial expenses.

One more loophole we need to plug as surely it will become greatly abused in the light of these other changes: Congressional Side Jobs. You know, extra income they might earn from book deals, speaking engagements, and even sitting on the board of directors for various corporations. These are just other ways to put envelopes full of money into your representative's back pocket. So, no. While you are serving as U.S. Senator or member of the House of Representatives, your sole source of compensation should come from the taxpayers. Period. (Notice I deliberately did not say all *income*, knowing there are many who will have dividend income from previous investments of some sort. But that is not compensation for their current work/labor/efforts, and of course, would need to be monitored closely.) If you want to do those other things for extra money, leave and re-enter the private sector. As a representative of the people, you should never forget who you truly work for.

The whole point, the WHOLE point, of these actions concerning compensation and housing, is to keep the special interests just one more step apart from our congressmen's attentions… and back pockets. This is the first phase in re-establishing a government of the people, by the people and for the people.

And as long as we're at it, let's talk about political junkets and so called 'fact-finding missions.' Far too many of these turn into nothing but boondoggle vacations paid for by the taxpayers, or worse, some special interest group trying to buy your representative! Such trips are supposed to be reported as income if paid for by third parties, but I think we have been very lax on such things. Making all Congressional travel records public would be a good start at regulating this abuse. But as far as fact-finding missions, I doubt the validity of any congressional mission that makes one stop at a military base before flying on to the capitals of Europe, especially when all the friends and family come along for the ride and the open bar. Maybe in the future, these trips need to be made in military transports on a diet of MREs? That's when you'll know the facts are really worth finding.

Okay. If we follow along, we've kicked the dinosaurs out of the capital, redefined and refocused their job descriptions toward serving the people who elected them. We've also isolated them from the cash-rich special interests. Next there are a few pieces of much needed legislation this new body needs to enact immediately:

Number one is of course, the Constitutional Amendment that limits their term in office. I think by this point, that's a given. But there is other legislation we now need because we have lost sight of what makes us... us:

We need legislation crafted in congress, not in the courts, that declares: Corporations are *not* people. They never were and they never should have been considered as such. It only makes it possible for some very rich and controlling people to overreach their roles as citizens at the expense of *your* voice. They shouldn't donate to political campaigns (more on that one later!) nor should they weigh in on political issues that affect people. Corporations are paper, not people. Period!

We need legislation that revokes all laws giving varying criminal penalties that are dependent on the status or profession of the victim. Remember early on in this book, I mentioned that there are laws that make it a more severe crime to kill a Senator, a Congressman, a President, a policeman or a Judge. Remember: All men (and women) are created EQUAL. Murder is murder, period, end of subject. But the penalty protecting one class of citizen more than another is wrong. Every time we pass a law that says someone's life is worth *more*, we make someone else's life worth a little *less*. Crime and punishment should be doled out equally among all citizens of these United States regardless of career, social standing, economic worth, as well as race, creed and color.

We need a more secure form of voter registration. It has been a cliché for decades that in certain areas, the dead continue to vote. It's also important that only actual citizens who are registered are allowed to vote... and vote only once per election. We already need photo ID in order to drive a car, get a mortgage buy a gun, get married, use your health insurance, enroll in college, etc., why not to vote? Other countries do it and in many places in this country, local governments have required it for years. The only ones that could possibly be opposed to this are the ones intending to commit voter fraud. And we could use some stiffer penalties for that, too!

There's one more item on this list that is going to ruffle a lot of feathers. We need to reaffirm the Electoral College. Yes, I said that. The Electoral College is a *good* thing and I fear without it, we would fall back into all-out Civil War within one or two election cycles. Please, let me explain:

No one complained about the legitimacy of the Electoral College until Hilary Clinton lost an election where she actually appears to have won the majority of votes cast. (I beg you to remember the issues I raised above with both 'dead' and 'non-citizen' voters. That majority is within the margin of error.) I remember similar complaints, although none violent, in 1960 when Kennedy beat Nixon, but Nixon had the majority of the votes. It was the Electoral College that tipped that election, too. Now, for whatever reasons, the history of 1960 seems to have been rewritten with many claiming Nixon did *not* have a majority after all. (I also realize there are people who say the moon landing never happened nor did the Holocaust.) But I was there! It was talked about and it was quite the discussion at the time! And then Walter Cronkite said, "That's the way it is," and we turned that page of history and moved forward.

The value of the Electoral College is that it keeps us *united*. For a candidate to win the election, they must do well in a wide range of states stretched across the nation. It forces the candidates to visit, campaign and meet face to face with people in every state. Not only does the candidate have to sell their platform to *everyone*, it also gives the candidate a chance to see, first hand, the state of the union and hear the voices of people too soon forgotten. The Electoral College makes the election of the President more of a national consensus, rather than just a regional plurality.

Now, let me explain that one. It is often said, "A Democracy is where two wolves and a sheep vote on what to have for dinner." Remember, we are a Republic! ("And to the Republic, for which it stands..." Remember?) In a Republic, the rights of the sheep are protected. Now, if we put the election of the President up for a nation-wide, one man, one vote, regardless of where they live election, certain populous regions of the country would make all the decisions for the rest of us without any voice... and the losers would be dinner.

Example: It would be possible for a presidential candidate to only campaign say, in New York, California, Florida and a couple of major cities like Chicago. And with that, they could win the entire election! If they were behind in a poll, all they would have to do is go back directly to their base where they are the strongest and drum up more votes from the same famer's field, so to speak. They would never even have to set foot in the middle of the country, never visit the corn fields or the coal mines. And they could win with this strategy! They could even run on a platform that said people in New York, California, Florida and maybe another state or two, would never have to pay income taxes again! And how would they pay for it? Why, they'd double the taxes on everybody else! See how you could win a majority real easy? Do you also see how those disaffected states might decide to succeed from the Union and we would have Civil War all over again. It would be just like The Hunger Games with twelve districts and a ruling capital. We should keep the Electoral College…

Now, with these more basic decisions out of the way, the next *major* assignment for our new 'People's Congress' would be Campaign Finance Reform.

Does it really matter how big the campaign budget is and where it came from? Yes, it *all* matters! When it comes to political campaigns, *everything* matters! Especially when there is *so* much of it!

Does anyone else dread the election cycle? The endless TV and radio ads that completely saturate the airwaves, most of which are attack ads spreading mistruth and heavily spun misunderstanding in the name of some recently formed political action group the candidate claims to have no knowledge of, nor control over? Are we all tired of the ads telling us the opposing candidate secretly visited with space aliens while having an affair with a circus animal? Doesn't it seem they really do get that ridiculous? And has any such ad ever changed your mind and caused you to vote the other way? Think about that.

The unimaginably vast amount of money spent on political advertising is disgraceful! And the only people listening are those who are already over-the-top, fire-breathing, loyal. It's a waste! It's an offensive, blatantly open attempt at brain washing. But how do we stop it? We end it with *Campaign Finance Reform.*

First off, there is going to be more resistance to this one subhead in this book than there will be to any other, including the Term Limits part. Who doesn't want to change the way things are now? For one, the political parties who feel if they pump enough money into a local election, they can buy any seat in the House (or Senate). But for another, the media likes things the way they are. Face it, this is a huge, cash-rich boom time for anyone with advertising space or airtime to sell. Those with the money want more of it, so no... they don't want to change it.

But let's change it anyway: What if a political candidate could only spend campaign funds that were actually raised by their *own* campaign *within* their *own* district? Let's say that again so it soaks in. What if politicians could only spend campaign funds donated by people who actually live and vote in the same district they are running to represent? And then what if we put a realistic cap on the total donation any individual can make? We don't need the rich donating to every single Congressional race across the country... just one! Any more than one is just buying influence.

I already said earlier that corporations are not people. So there can be no corporate or special interest group donations. None! Nada! And let's extend that to political parties and other special interest groups, too. A political party should not be allowed to hold $15,000 per plate dinners/fundraisers on one side of the country, and then flood that money into small, local races in the backwaters of America. That's not 'Free Speech,' that's bribery and propaganda. There should be no 'Super Pacs' or any political action groups financially involved in any campaign. When we allowed that to happen, it was a perversion of the First Amendment. Big special interest organizations should not be allowed to open their big checkbooks either and 'buy' a vote on future legislation. And this goes right back to the idea at the beginning, that you as an individual can't afford to get your own representative's attention. You don't have enough money. This way... you *do*!

Those steps right there are going to *greatly* reduce political advertising! It's going to force each and every candidate to make every dollar they spend count... and they will probably want to spend what time they *can* buy, telling you about themselves, and what they want to do if elected. They would probably have no money left over for those attack ads about space aliens and affairs with circus animals. Wouldn't that be a plus! It's going to boil those campaigns right down to the basics of "who I am and what I stand for," rather than what some slick advertising guy can get you to believe. (And I know, I used to be a slick advertising guy!)

It's also going to greatly reduce the power of the political parties themselves. (And they are going to fight like hell to stop this!) It's going to greatly limit the places these party bosses can spend the money they raise and then hopefully, greatly reduce the money the wealthy will feel compelled to give them. The parties will return to a much earlier role of 'like-thinking individuals meeting to agree on common goals" and the days of the all-powerful, unelected political machine will go the way of Tammany Hall.

A final thought here, though one that will never come to fruition: Think of the good we could do with all that wasted campaign money spent on attack ads and lies. Think of the people we could feed, the diseases we could cure and the youth, *our* youth, we could educate. I guess we'll just have to find some other way to get that money back in circulation and not stagnating at the top of the economy.

It's time to do some tax adjusting: If you were paying attention in the first part of this book, you already know that Income Disparity is a real problem in the United States these days. And while everyone complains about them, taxes are not truly, fairly apportioned across our vast income ranges. Did you know that at one time, the high-income tax bracket was a whopping ninety percent? I have to agree, there indeed was something to complain about. A tax that large could be smothering to any economy. But these days, those with the money and the influence over your representatives have dialed that top bracket back to a mere thirty-seven percent (after various deductions and exclusions). And then, you have to make more than a half a million dollars a year (about six-hundred-thousand dollars if filing jointly) to even touch that bracket.

What's even better (if you're this well-paid), is that you only have to pay Social Security taxes on the first $132,900 you make, and that's up nearly five grand from last year. It's called 'The Cap' and somewhere, a long time ago, this came into play. What's that mean? It means all those huge salaries, all those mammoth bonuses we hear about, are virtually exempt from paying into Social Security, a government benefit we are constantly told is going broke!

How do we save Social Security? Very simple: First, we prevent Congress from ever again reaching into the Social Security Trust Fund whenever they're running short, and *then*, we eliminate the Social Security Tax Cap. With every dollar earned in the United States subject to the tax (6.2% for the employer and another 6.2% for the employee for a total of 12.4%), Social Security would have instant solvency and I dare say, quite a surplus! Why... we could even double the current Social Security payments and still come out ahead. Let me repeat that: We need to double the Social Security payments to Seniors and the disabled and we can easily afford to do that and *more* by eliminating the Social Security Tax Cap.

We have a similar issue with Medicare taxes although there is no income cap on this deduction, but more on that in a bit. The important takeaway here, is that by eliminating a couple of cleverly placed loopholes and readjusting a few tax brackets that were placed only to benefit the well-off, there is so much we could do here at home without ever stepping across that allegedly evil line of socialism! Here is a hard truth: The 'Haves' have scared the 'Have-nots' into thinking that anything less than what they (the 'Haves') have right now, is stepping off some cliff into a Soviet-styled socialism and would be the end of the world. The truth is, there is a whole lot of wiggle room in the middle and the 'Have-nots' are holding the short end of the stick. (Well, maybe not the 'short' end, but it is spelled much the same!) For the future of this country, we need to rebalance that a bit. Think of the things we could do if we all paid a fair portion of taxes, corporations included.

Lets start by setting ourselves on a course to close the Income Disparity gap. With tax structures as they are now, the wealthiest Americans and Corporations (here, Corporations actually *do* count as people.) find it beneficial to first, maximize their profits and then, re-invest, shelter, and stash that cash in the upper levels of the economic ladder. Money makes money. Invested money makes even more money... for those who hold the investments. There is currently very little incentive to divert a deserving portion of these profits back down the tax brackets to rank and file workers. In fact, many of these employers abused the system and maximized profits by freezing pay structures and cutting benefits. And then they reduced many people's employment status to part-time, so they didn't have to pay benefits at all. But profits were up and times were good... just like in the 1920s! (That's back in the part of the book many of you have burned by now.)

[57]

There are two things to understand here: *First,* what if we were to readjust upper income tax structures so there was a larger pool of taxable monies, and then add a financial penalty to hording, stashing and inequitably sharing that surplus. Then, at the same time, offer tax breaks and credits for reinvesting in their own payroll at levels, lets say, below a hundred-thousand dollars annually. If we did *that,* those at the top of the financial structure are going to have to give up a noticeably larger portion of the profits than before, either way. One way, they go out the door to the government never to be seen again. The other way, they are investing in their *own* people, raising wages, closing that income gap and in the end, getting a better quality of employee. (They go to the highest bidder, too!)

Now, for those of you demanding that $15/hour minimum wage, this is a path to get there. But it *also* comes with the responsibility to *act* like a much more valued employee! You have to be worthy of it! It took years, decades for us to get to such a level of Income Disparity. It will take quite some time for it to balance out as well. There are no quick fixes.

The *second* thing to consider here is that it will change the face of American commerce. There will be some businesses that will thrive under these new rules. And there will be those that simply won't make it. If they don't make it, it's due to their own business model.

Now, for those of you who may not know what a business model is, it's basically a formula that says, 'Hey, we can buy raw burgers for this, condiments are an expense, and we need a building to serve them in. We also need workers to flip and serve these things. If we buy for this price, and hire at that wage… we can make a profit of X amount of dollars.' It doesn't matter what the industry is, there's a business model. If the model works, they will stay in business. If not, they and the jobs will be gone. There will be those businesses, *any* type of business, that will flourish in this environment. There will be those that will fail if the balance of cash flow is too abruptly altered. Then there will be those who will find their model no longer works at all.

My best example of that may sound crude and extreme, but please think of this as a business lesson. Let's look at the cotton industry in the years before the Civil War. Every plantation owner could calculate that with this much land, that much labor, he could produce X amount of cotton. And with the price of cotton, (plus the cost of processing it and transporting it to market), he could make a profit! Obviously, some made *big* profits. The only problem with this business model is that it was entirely dependent on slave labor!

After the Civil War, when faced with the reality of paying their labor force (either in some form of wage or a share of the crop), with the cost of production and the price of cotton, their business model failed! Plantations not lost during the war itself, soon went back to the banks and were re-allocated as smaller farms. The cotton industry was crippled and it took years, decades for it to fully recover through improved technology in agriculture, and in the processing and transportation supply chains.

I bring this example to your attention *only* to say that there will be some businesses today that have cut the margins too thin, who found their niche too close to the edge and will not survive any such economic shift. (It would be like building a beach house at low tide.) They will be gone. But don't fear, those that prosper will expand their employment ranks to fill the void, and there will be new business, new opportunities that will find new niches in a more balanced economy.

Now, just as I cautioned the workers to be worthy of rising wages. I need to caution the employer against seeing a fixed profit pool. What that means is if someone were to say, open five fast food restaurants (or car dealerships or insurance offices) owners do the math and say, 'That's X amount of profit every year! *My* profit!' Sometimes, they tend to see that as a guaranteed pool of profit, that *their* share comes first. If an economic setback or adjustment intervenes, they tend to see the solution in a price increase, a wage or labor cut, anything that leaves their profit pool untouched and puts any irregularity on the pocketbooks of someone else. That's where you hear the arguments about increasing the minimum wage will create $17 hamburgers and robotic order takers. It's just someone making threats to protect their personal profit pool. We need to let the business models sort them out, not fear.

You know, if nothing else, I hope you are seeing that so very many of the things that affect our lives are hopelessly interconnected. You just can't focus on solving this problem or that one over there. One balances another and while we do need to move carefully, we *do* need to *move*, and move in a different direction than we have been heading. I'm, afraid these last few subheads are going to be the most hopelessly interconnected of them all. Sorry.

[59]

Healthcare: For a modern, industrialized nation, our healthcare industry is in a truly sad state with only one real cause: Greed. We have millions of people who can't get health insurance, can't afford it, and with rising deductibles, co-pays and coinsurance fees, (no, those are NOT the same thing and you are billed separately!), the insurance many of us have access to, is pretty much useless. (I went through this recently as I personally needed to bridge the gap between retirement and Medicare eligibility.)

Too many people, especially our senior citizens, are just one major illness away from complete financial collapse. Hospitals are expensive and while I wish I could say they only 'nickel and dime' you, the billing process has become a high-stakes minefield of hidden consultation fees and ten-dollar aspirins with extra, extra charges for dozens of lab fees, X-rays and overlapping procedures. And then there are the skyrocketing costs for medications and all the pharmaceutical reps you see in the hallways. Doctors are expensive because of the exorbitant malpractice insurance they are compelled to buy, and pass the cost along to you. And that falls on all the underemployed lawyers we talked about much earlier. (Again, this whole book is my own personal opinion.)

So what do we do? In every subhead so far, I have suggested a possible cure for that specific ill. (No pun intended). But across our Healthcare industry, there is such abuse, such corruption, such profiteering, I fear they have lost all faith in the eyes of the American people and the relationship is irreparable. Long before Martin Shkreli bought the patent on a common aids drug and jacked the price from $13.50 to $750 per pill and then laughed about it on national television, long before he became known as 'the most hated man in America...' long before that, the relationship with the healthcare and pharmaceutical industries was hopelessly broken. I see no cure here but nationalization of a major part of these industries. This is not the way me, the Capitalist would like to see things go, but the sad truth is, we will *never*, ever have affordable healthcare as long as there are guys with three-thousand dollar suits walking around in our healthcare system. They were given the chance to be responsible business citizens, and they abused it *and* the people they were said to be caring for.

Come on, we *are* that modern, industrialized nation, that shining city on the hill, and we are rich (as a nation). There is no reason we cannot adopt and deploy an effective national healthcare system. What's more, it's high time we did so! Yes, there will be those who scream 'socialism' and 'the end of the world' offering 'proof' of 'death-boards' and falsified facts from other 'failed' countries. They'll tell you that's what's coming if you do this. So let me tell you a story from my own life here:

In the mid 1990s, I was in a serious car accident that left me with a damaged left hip joint. Suddenly, I was no longer able to cross that leg, or even put on a sock without severe, arthritic-like pain. At the time, I was insured through an HMO that 'managed' my healthcare. I was in their mega-clinic building, seeing my doctor who wanted to see what was going on inside this joint. He wanted to send me out for an MRI but needed plan approval. In a clinic this size, plan approval was just down the hall… practically across the hall from the exam room where I waited. My doctor failed to close the door to the exam room (perhaps on purpose?) and went to seek the necessary signature. I could hear… I could *hear* every word that went on in that room as my doctor requested approval for an MRI and the 'Plan Administrator' made every excuse *not* to approve it! He even questioned at 'my age' what quality of life would this expense bring to me. I was just over forty years old at the time! At 'my age' I should just suffer with it?

Well, I have always been an A-type personality and I got up off that table and followed the voices across the hall. When I got there, I gave a very large piece of my mind, at more than significant volume, to this very stunned Plan Administrator. Long story short, I got my signature and several weeks later, arthroscopic hip surgery that literally changed my life. But if I hadn't overheard that conversation… I would have suffered these past twenty-five years. So, you fear that some form of national healthcare is going to take decisions away from your doctor and give you 'death-boards?' I'm telling you, you've got them already! And it's time to change that! But as long as big money insurance and pharmaceuticals can influence your Congressman's vote, it won't. Until we can take back our Congress with term limits and campaign finance reform, it never will.

Yes, I know, with any kind of national healthcare there will be bugs to work out like they found in Britain. Yes, it could be much better managed than the Canadians have done, but there are other countries where it works financially, and it works for the betterment of the people. Think of it like

[61]

Medicare... for all. A phrase we have heard a lot in the last couple of years, but one the dinosaurs in Washington who have overstayed their time... have blocked.

There will be those within the industry who will cry foul, unfair, and who will call a whole bunch of scary lawyers into the fight. I beg to remind them, during the French Revolution, being a profiteer on the backs of the public was enough to get you declared 'an enemy of the people,' and they had certain guillotines set aside JUST for these criminals where the blades were said to be slightly blunted. But as long as we are building a gallows behind the Capital Building anyway... if it comes to that... well, there's always room for one more!

So where do we start? Healthcare is a multi-layer, cause-and-effect problem. We need to start at the top and work our way down.

First, we need to consolidate Medicare Parts A, B & D into one comprehensive healthcare program. Then we need to extend availability of that very same program to every U.S. citizen regardless of age, race, creed, color, economic background, natural citizen, naturalized citizen, etc. Everybody is cared for the same from ghetto-born baby to President of United States. Everybody. If you can't get it in Wilbur, Washington, you can't get it in Washington D.C., either... especially on the floor of the Senate! (Do this and see how fast that 'Doughnut Hole' coverage gap gets closed. Everyone on Medicare knows what I mean. Ask them.)

Next, with the private insurance companies nearly out of existence, or at least with a very reduced role, we will need Medicare to negotiate pharmaceutical prices with the manufacturers. And since there would be only one government buying office, we can demand much fairer pricing. Yes, they are going to yell and scream they can't do research and development nor proper distribution without price protections. But they seem to let everyone one else around the world have it at a pretty good deal. And personally, I think the united leverage of a national healthcare system could do even better.

We will need to be prepared for a slowdown, if not a halt in the research of vital cures and drugs. A fact I am sure they will let us know about in every detail. But eventually, they will get back to business as usual as soon as they find they don't have to have those twenty-eight-million dollar bonuses passed out to the three-thousand dollar suit club. Once those dinosaurs are extinct, we will be well on the road to a government-funded healthcare that our tax dollars can genuinely provide.

But watch out for this pitfall as I promise you it will come: There will be offered a compromise where as the National Healthcare Plan will wind-up watered-down in its coverage and to get the care you *really* need, you will still need to purchase a private insurance 'supplement' plan... so you will still need the insurance executives. Then, over time, the national plan will cover less and less, and the supplement will pick up the slack, but charge you more, and more. Please, if you are brave enough to stand up and fight for this, don't settle for half. When it comes to this, there is no compromise.

The next stumbling block will be our doctors' cost of doing business. Malpractice insurance may also have to be nationalized and that won't happen until we harness the wild, rogue lawyers! We need what is called 'tort reform' or a cap and limit on medical malpractice suits. Having an unsuccessfully resolved medical issue is *not* the same as hitting the lotto! And we have to stop treating it as such. If we can greatly reduce the number and cap the settlements of malpractice insurance claims, doctors can afford to treat us as people again, not as liabilities. Hospitals would no longer have to run endless, redundant tests in order to cover their own butts in potential law suits. All of this will bring the cost of healthcare tumbling down. We just have to eliminate the unbridled access to our wallets that Insurance Execs, Pharmaceutical companies, and Lawyers have turned into their own windfall retirement plans.

But while we're talking about limiting lawyers, let's extend that tort reform and liability cap to cover auto insurance, slip and fall, and anything else you would chase an ambulance for. We need fewer lawyers on TV telling us how they just won someone the biggest settlement in history... and how "you could be next!" It will take time to turn the tide on this out-of-control industry. But remember, it took us a good fifty years to screw it up as much as we have, it will take time to change attitudes, opinions and improve the situation. It may never be 'fixed.'

Education: And now, the last healthcare stumbling block actually leads us into the next topic. Our educational system is as equally screwed up as our healthcare system. And let's start from the doctors' point of view:

[63]

Ever wonder why it seems you can't pronounce your own doctor's name anymore? Whatever happened to 'Dr. Smith,' 'Dr. Baker' or even 'Dr. Janakowski?' What happened is those three guys couldn't afford the rising costs of a college education and medical school! They got caught in the Income Disparity gap and their ability to pay for such things was outstripped. So... they never happened. Mr. Smith, Ms. Baker and that Janakowski guy may very well be the orderly who took care of you in the hospital, or the paramedic who saved your life after the car accident. One of them may even be the pharmaceutical rep we talked about in the section above. But in *this* section, the important thing is they were prevented from following a dream and never became doctors.

But where did the doctors we *do* have come from? Many came from third-world nations with thick accents that make them hard to understand. They came on student visas to become doctors and then stayed in the United States. While I am not opposed to any form of legal immigration, I will raise the question as to how these individuals could afford the education our own, homegrown sons and daughters could not? In many cases... they didn't have to pay. Between grants and scholarships from our government and programs specifically designed to aid these third-world students, they were able to afford to take the place of, Drs Smith, Baker, and Janakowski.

But it's just not medical school. If you were born and raised here, you face a tremendous uphill battle seeking higher education of any kind. Somehow, education became a commodity that gets sold to the highest bidder and something so valuable, people are even willing to bribe and cheat their way to the head of the line regardless of academic qualifications. Many of those that *do* find a way through and survive the lack of help we give our *own* people, are saddled with a life-time of debt from student loans.

Wake up! We are a nation, not a marketplace. We are still competing in an international race! We compete every day with the best engineers, research scientists, doctors, mathematicians, and physicists the rest of the world has trained. They took their best and brightest and set them on a path to discovery for the betterment of their people and at some price, the rest of us. At that same time, *we* were educating those who had the most means and whose parents knew the right people, regardless if they had even passed their SATs. And we charged them all for the privilege of being there... with interest.

If we want to be there for the Space Race, the Tech Race, the Arms Race, The Race for the Cure, if we want to be there for all that and so much *more*, we need to start taking our best and brightest and treating them as an asset, not a commodity. We need to identify these people and make certain every opportunity is there for them as they, in every sense of the word, will represent us.

Make no mistake about it, this means free educational opportunities (and this is the important part) to *those who have proven worthy*. That's *not*, those who are more disadvantaged, those who need a more level playing field, those from a long-established family tree or those from a selected ethnic background. It would be for those who could actually help us *win* these all important races!

Now, if there is room left over (and I am certain there will be lots), then, you can buy your way in, then you can promote social opportunity programs, then you can set up specialized scholarships. But the first seats are free and go to the most deserving based on previous academic achievement regardless of economic or social status. You can thank me later, Dr. Baker…

We need to eliminate all student debt. Making our young people into indentured servants for our banking industry is… shall I be nice and say 'not culturally advanced.' With revised tax structures and lots of special interest money no longer wasted buying congressional votes or elections, there should be lots of available funds corporations could be convinced into investing in scholarships and trades programs. Think of it this way Mr. Chairman of the Board, why buy off a Congressman when you can invest in several future, home-grown VPs of your own? Eliminating existing Student Debt, by scaled-down payment plans, zero interest loans, government grants, or outright amnesty should be a goal we could compare to Jesus chasing those moneylenders from the Temple thing mentioned above.

We need to make our skilled trades important again. We not only need to be a nation of thinkers and engineers, but we need to be a nation of *builders*. We need to make things like our grandfathers again. And you can build nothing without skilled tradesmen. But somewhere we got lost. We lost pride in a perfect weld, a straight wall and a solid road to anywhere we dreamed of going. After high school, somehow, it became college… or burger flipping, with nothing in between. We need those builders back if we will ever rebuild this country! (And please, start with our failing infrastructure!)

[65]

But as long as we are talking about education, and I just mentioned high school, we are truly off the rails when we look what happened to our public education system. What used to be a model for the civilized world has become a baby-sitting service, mired in its own misplaced best efforts. I am from a family of public school educators and administrators and remember well not only what I learned in school, but what my father, a public school superintendent taught me *about* school... and it's something we have all forgotten. This part may sound rather sexist at first, but remember, it's the way things *were*, and it's a reference point you can build on, not abandon. All ideas can be adapted.

The original intent of the Public School System was to prepare the children of the community to replace their parents within that same community. It was to prepare the next generation to carry on. And by bringing the children together to all be taught the same thing at the same place instead of through a community of Home Schoolers, it assured they would all start life on as equal a footing as possible.

There were a lot of lessons built into the structure that had nothing to do with the classes on Reading, Writing and Arithmetic. From the earliest years, this is where we all learned there were others, just like us in our world... classmates. We learned social skills through games, class activities, and following a structure. We did and learned things together, as a group. We all said the Pledge of Allegiance every morning, together, and we learned about loyalty and unity, and that there would be 'Liberty and Justice for all.' It was our first taste of being part of something bigger than ourselves.

As we progressed through the grades, we were put into social situations that required a higher order of social skills like, how to ask a girl to the dance, how to accept or decline that invitation, how to behave at that dance, and we certainly all learned that boys don't think like girls and that girls most definitely don't think like boys. We were in clubs and organizations that had structure and a division of labor that needed teamwork if there was going to be an Annual that year or a Science Club campout that month.

Our school became a microcosm of the world. Some kids joined band or choir and added to other organized social functions we attended. (Imagine Graduation without the band!) Some of us played sports and if you made the team, you were the best 'our school' had to offer and even if you rode the spectator bus, you learned that *they* represented *you* against 'the bad guys.'

[66]

Everybody was encouraged to pursue and develop their talents. All of us had a very solid taste of what it was like to be part of something bigger than ourselves, and to be loyal to and a citizen of, our very own hometown community.

The lessons continued to become more and more advanced. Prom was there not just because a bunch of girls thought it would be fun to have a dress-up and play grown-up night. It taught us all, prepared us all, for life's events we would surely face someday. Fumbling with that Tuxedo and those shirt studs? That spaghetti-strapped dress and corsage? Prom was your training ground because someday, it would be your wedding, and if your wedding wasn't that fancy, there was a good chance your daughter's might be. There were other social skills learned that night that involved eating in public without storing snacks in your cummerbund, how to treat your date as if you were in a real, grown-up relationship. Remember, Prom wasn't just some other dance, or a night at the basketball game. It meant committing to go with each other, coordinating your clothes, and being considerate of your partner to make the relationship work… if only for one night. Asking a girl to Prom was the most important decision and stress-related thing you would do shy of your marriage proposal. And waiting for the 'right' guy to ask, or choosing the offer you had, was just as important for those on the other team. There were a lot of lessons in high school the teachers never graded you on, these are only *some* of them.

Let me throw in one, out of place thought here. These days, many parents don't want their teenager making a single commitment to 'a' prom date. They seem to like them 'unattached' and sadly inexperienced in such matters until they are older. Many sigh a great relief when they all decide to go to Prom as 'a group date.' No one asked anybody, just a social click went as a group. Well, it's only Prom, it's not marriage or anything.

However, a group date denies them the lessons mentioned here about dealing with stress, learning the social order of things, the proper behavior, the *practice* for when they grow up! You don't want your kid to approach marriage with the same unstressed approach as that, do you? Marriage is not a group date! But… with the divorce rate these days and the lack of commitment to their partners we see, maybe these were the lessons they learned instead. Now, back to talking about the good old days:

[67]

But academics became more important in later high school as well. Your school board and educators knew that after graduation, many would be suddenly faced with entirely grown-up problems and realities. Only the first one would be marriage. To keep these relationships together, to make family units function, the schools taught those girls how to feed their families and make their clothes because many would indeed be homemakers. In shop classes, the boys learned how to fix the house, repair the car, and build things that could make family life run a little smoother. These were the basic skills that were taught us and before you start to shout 'Sexist,' 'Chauvinist' or that one that starts with an 'M' I don't want to even learn how to spell... before you do that, know this: At my advanced age, I know people I went to high school with who did indeed go on to college, onto to careers, who set records and broke barriers who *still*, after all these years, still make references to industrial arts or home arts skills they learned in that societal microcosm called high school. No matter how liberal or conservative you are, no matter how many copies of this book you have already burned, these were important lessons we taught our kids in those days. And you know what? They should still be so today!

So where did it get off track? Well, go back and read that Income Disparity section at the very beginning of this book. Remember, I told you it was all interrelated and none of our problems stand alone. But specific to high school, Greed and Income Disparity lie at the bottom of things.

Schools need money, they get money through taxes and working people pay those taxes. But as the economy grew tighter for some, they couldn't afford more taxes and started voting down millage elections and bond issues. The schools were cash strapped. Programs were cut starting with the music and the arts. As the grandson of a pretty damn good band director, I'll tell you, music is important. Yes, it adds to the social microcosm of high school in many ways, but even more important, not everyone 'thinks' with the same process. Our brains are all wired differently and music not only teaches group skills, but it teaches you to think outside of the box, so to speak. It's math and logic taught from another angle. Both music and art teach the student other avenues of problem-solving. That keeps us all from just being regurgitating machines, believe it or not, and later in life, more than one opinion on how to solve a problem could literally be a life saver.

Sports were the next to be cut, many programs being saved only by 'pay to play' schemes where you could go out for a sport only if your parents could afford to pay for your participation, and afford the time to organize and participate in fund raising events.

These cuts and changes were the beginning of the end to so many of the important lessons the Public School structure had taught in the past. It was no longer, 'our' team or 'our' band and we no longer fielded the very best our school had to offer. Suddenly it was 'elitist' and we were sending the 'rich kids' to cheer for the 'spoiled jocks' while the 'band brats' marched on. And while they may have covered the financial cost of this, the real cost was our unity.

When there's less to aspire to, even in the younger grades, aspirations will start to fall short. No one wants to participate. They are only in it for themselves. And sadly, that's an attitude also held by many of their teachers. A second generation of disaffected students is now telling their own kids they don't have to do this or that, or stand for this or participate in that. The parent and the teacher are no longer on the same side and just like in any divorce, the child caught in the middle has learned how to manipulate the situation to his or her own advantage. We are no longer teaching, we are babysitting some of the most selfish, demanding, entitled little monsters the world has seen since the French and Russian revolutions combined. Don't believe me? Sign up to be a substitute teacher for just one day. And if that's too much, go along as a chaperone on a field trip.

"Quickly," the substitute teacher demanded, "How do we fix it?" Sorry, there is no 'quick' about it. There is no sequential order. You just have to roll up your sleeves, jump in, and start to put things back on the shelves.

First, return discipline to our public schools. There is nothing as un-teachable as bratty kid (of any age less than 18), who knows they don't have to do what you say and aren't afraid to taunt you about it. That means we have to get parents back on the side of the school districts so that we can return to the days of 'the punishment I got as school is nothing like I will get when I get home!' Two generations of parents have now decided their little darlings are perpetually faultless and it's the teacher and their accomplice, that F*&@%$ Principal behind it all.

To change this we could well start with body cams throughout the schools and busses. This will do much to show these oppositional-combative parents what charmers their little angels truly are. At the same time, knowing they are being recorded is often the biggest deterrent to bad behavior. To add to that, I would beseech these parents to bite their tongues, and wait to see what changes a little discipline in school might make at home, too. If this is still insufficient, there are other alternatives. I am certain that down the road from their house someplace there will be another school run by a burly nun with a ruler. Try that one for a while. Regardless, none of us can any longer sacrifice the many lessons our children could be learning at the cost of *your* child's non-compliance and disruptive attitude. Sorry. Shoot me.

Here's a chance for the other side to take a shot at me, too. In order to bring the parents full circle as to be on the same side as their school district, we need accountability at the big desk in the room. Face it, there is nothing that has more affect on your child (again, of any age), nothing that will be longer remembered, than a dedicated teacher shaping the lives of their students. Nothing except for one thing, the only thing more memorable or more influential. And that's a teacher who no longer gives a crap and is marking time to retirement (whether it is five years or twenty-five years).

I mentioned I did some substitute teaching at one point in my life. The only thing more shocking to me than the attitudes of some of these little monsters (truly, I am being generous), are the actions and the attitudes of some of the teachers I met in the lounge over lunch periods. I saw teachers bitching, complaining, mimicking selected difficult students and setting up a pre-dispositioned attitude with the teacher that student would have next year. "He's a disrespectful handful and he's coming your way!" Read between the lines, your kid is doomed to a label and the failure that comes with him or her before next year ever starts!

I saw teachers, mostly the older ones, berate and bully the younger ones concerning union votes and even political elections. I saw more than one in more than one teachers lounge, demand to know who this or that one was going to vote for in a national election... and then publically criticize, ridicule and condemn that choice. Now, before you jump to conclusions, the teachers I am telling you about were proud, button busting... liberals! And the election in question, my time in the teachers' lounge, was well over twenty-five years ago. Yet, these *same* teachers, not afraid to bully their own co-workers against the school administration and any Republican candidate, were the very same people 'teaching' your children about the evils of bullying and the zero tolerance policy against any form of violence. And you wonder why it's not working.

Yes, Parents need to have faith in the school district, and have patience while things change. But teachers need to clean up their ranks as well. And by the way, those that are still teaching after the herd is thinned need to be paid a lot more than we currently give them. But then, you get what you pay for.

If we can all get on that same page, actually bring discipline back into schools, and we can find a way to fund the extracurricular activities again and make them available to all, then and only then, can we start bringing back those other important life lessons and values. And whether college bound or marriage and an apprenticeship awaits, these lessons are all a good base to start from. I'm certain you have some thoughts of your own. Some of them may involve me and your ACME catalog. But let me ask you to at least consider these ideas. Now, it's time to move on to our international problems, our foreign policy, and our military. Turn the page.

America Vs The World: It started in the days after World War II. Virtually all of Europe lay in rubble then but it was still the hub of international commerce and finance at that time. We *needed* to rebuild Europe so all the world could function again.

Mistakes were made. Yes, we rebuilt buildings and infrastructure, but we also created nations that hadn't existed before, too often clumping groups of people that didn't like each other together under one flag in the name of efficiency. And this saddled us with the term 'Nation Building' which sadly seems to have been our military and foreign policy ever since.

Every war, military action, or 'defensive positioning' since then couldn't garner enough support in Congress unless it came with the guilty promise that we would stick around after the invasion and fix what we bombed. It was now our responsibility to help them set up a democratic government just like ours, and then let the presence of our troops insure fare elections of a government favorable to us. That would make it alright, see? All the while, our most earnest helpers would come in and teach these poor people how to live and properly exist in the desert or barren mountain range where their ancestors had lived for thousands of years.

Point of information, 'nation building' means 'occupation.' And even the mobs of teary-eyed people who greeted us as liberators across Europe in the 1940s, eventually *tired* of being occupied and told how to live. It's left us with our troops spread across the globe and a world-wide network of military bases to support as 'they keep the peace.'

You ever wonder why so many people around the world hate us? Why they will reach across thousands of miles from around the globe to defame us, even attack us? It's because they don't like being occupied. They don't like being told how to live or structure their society and they may not even *want* to be like us. But we're not giving them much of a choice, are we?

As unpopular as it will be, we need to change the nature of this foreign policy to something much more 'hit and run.' If another regime threatens us, and by that I don't mean just saying bad things about us, I mean actually *threatens* our safety, our well-being be it by violent attacks on our people and homeland, or attacks on ships under our flag at sea, or in some other way, infringing on our commerce and right to exist in our own space. If we are genuinely *threatened*, we will, as always, retaliate. But rather than occupy and build housing and water mains and English-speaking schools, we need to take care of business, eliminate the threat and then *leave*. We need to leave them sitting in their own rubble.

With the technology and tools our military has today, we can keep the great majority of our troops at *home*, and then rapidly deploy them and any weapons they need to any point on Earth in frighteningly short order. If someone poses a legitimate threat, we quickly attack, as surgically as possible destroy the objective and then leave them to their own devices. No occupation! It could take an evil, rogue government like the Taliban *years* to crawl out of their caves and recover from such a pan-caking. If and when they do regain power and control of their population again, we simply repeat the pan-cake procedure. I do believe we will find it is cheaper and less costly in American lives to flatten them twice than to occupy them over the same amount of time. Also remember, every time they get pan-caked, they are suddenly on an equal par with the people whose rights they trampled when taking power. When suddenly sitting in the same pile of rubble, things change.

If you're following, we will save a tremendous amount of tax dollars by reducing our military presence on a world-wide scale. Also, over time, we will not need to maintain a military the same size we currently do. We currently have an excessive military budget and that's not even considering the vast amounts of money we give away overseas simply trying to buy friends and influence people. But these reductions along with some other 'common sense' defense and State Department cutbacks, could mean we would be able to reduce costs *and* better support the military we *do* have. And that means two things:

First, we could spend a lot more money on the VA and caring for those who have sacrificed in service to our country. I understand from those I know that things have been getting better since the days of lost appointment lists and doctor appointments scheduled after your life expectancy, but we still have a very long way to go to get these people the care they need and the respect they deserve. Perhaps with these policy changes and budget reallocations, we could do what's right.

The only thing worse than the way we treat our veterans, is the way we treat those currently in uniform. Have you looked at military pay scales lately? Many who are married, exist on food stamps and that is an out and out disgrace! We ask them for total commitment, 24/7, to lay their very lives on the line to defend our freedom, but we pay them like completely unskilled labor. I'm sorry, but I cannot help but think of the hypocrisy of the ruling class rattling their jewelry in Washington, and in essence telling our enemies "Straighten up and do it our way, or we will send our peasants to beat up your peasants... you know, the ones we feed with food stamps."

With proper budget reallocations, reduced military spending and increased tax revenue; we should have no problem doubling the pay of each and every member of our armed forces. Read that again, we should double all military pay so that no one in uniform needs to ever see a food stamp, a Bridge card, or any form of public economic assistance again! Now, to all you Washington types who laughed at the idea of an armed insurrection that would chase you and your special interests from the halls of the Capital Building. All those that said the military would of course be on your side during any such civil unrest and suppress the people should they decide to take up arms. Tell, me... how confident do you feel about all that now?

Closing Statements

So, what do we do now? First, I think we all need to take stock of our current situations and give careful consideration to the ideas presented here. I hope, by grouping these issues together and taking a fresh look at that 'Big Picture,' I have helped you all to see things from another perspective, to at least consider causes and alternatives. And even if I have not altered your position, I hope you are at least now more aware of the plight of others.

To move forward successfully, we *all* need to give up our political party loyalties, not just in the voting booths, but in our daily lives and even in our Internet arguments. This is not some college rivalry where we wear the school colors, chant the cheers and stand by our team through thick and thin. We need to stop letting a party affiliation be part of our self-identities. (Remember, we are not supposed to work *for* them, but they for *us*!) There is *no* room for "Democrats forever!" or, "Republicans know best!" No, "Their team is all lying scumbags!" regardless of what party pin that scumbag may wear.

Actually, there is a lot of truth in that last statement… they are *all* lying scumbags! (Boy, that felt good!) But I hope I've shown you, over time, how *both* sides have deceived, misled and manipulated you and your vote into quietly handing your prosperity over to them. They comfortably hold all the cards and will do anything to keep things as they are.

There is a great cancer killing our nation and it resides in the halls of Congress. The only cure, the very first thing that needs to change, the one thing that prevents all other change, is Congressional Term Limits. While I am not proposing out and out revolution, I most definitely think there needs to be a 'purge' whereby anyone who has been in the House or the Senate more than twelve years is convinced to leave immediately, by whatever means it takes. Their respective state governors have the power to appoint replacements for them who may either, finish out their predecessor's term in office, or hold that seat until a special election can decide things.

Worse than the elected officials who have stayed too long, are the un-elected Power Brokers. You know who I mean and they do too. That would include the party bosses who are actually making the decisions and the

[75]

special interest who are buying the influence you can't afford. As soon as the power structure in Congress is shifted by removing the career politicians, those relationships will become exposed.

This is going to take a combined, united stand by the *people*, without concern for party, and without the fear that one party will use this to advance on the other's position. Democrat-people have as much reason to want this change as do Republican-people. If you fail to see this at this point, go back to page one and start over again!

What it will take: Any such action is going to create great turmoil in Washington that will echo down to each and every state capitol. But we must also remember that we are a significant force in stabilizing the current global situation. A failure of our government could unleash aggression across the globe "now that the Sherriff's out of town." It could also open our own nation to foreign attack as our enemies might see a weakened government as an opportunity to settle old issues. In fact, one point further, those who would oppose any change to the current system will use these arguments as a reason to leave well enough alone. Remember that one!

To make this 'purge' happen while retaining our sovereignty and some level of world peace, we would need a very strong President. He or she would have to be one who has no real vested interest or loyalty to either party, one who could keep the government functioning on a day to day basis while the legislative branch undergoes "renovations and personnel replacement." It *could* all happen very quickly and very painlessly over a single time period when Congress is not in session anyway. But if those who have over-stayed their welcome refuse to step down, it could take a little longer, but still end in the very same result.

Either way, once Congress is fully staffed again, all can return to the 'normal' as seen by the Founding Fathers. That very strong President will then have to be even stronger to relinquish any authority he may have exercised in that time period and *not* continue to advance his position. He would by then *have* to be aware that the very people who ousted the power brokers from the Capital Building are indeed, just down the street.

Are you afraid of risk? There is always safety in numbers, no one wants to be the first one to step up and ask, "please, sir, can I have some more?" But it has to be done and once done, becomes easier for every one that follows suit. Consider me that first one to step forward and I did so by sticking my own neck out to write this book. Remember, I'm just an old man living on Social Security somewhere in a seniors' trailer park. I don't have much, but then, I don't have much to lose.

When this book hits the streets, I am most assuredly going to be sued by people with far, far more than I have. I will be ridiculed for my positions, and detractors will attempt to discredit the things I have said due to anything from my spelling skills to the color of my hair. When they realize that Goliath suing David will only help book sales, they will attempt to stop distribution of the book on grounds of treason, inciting a riot, or something buried in the Terrorism act despite the First Amendment.

If they stop the book, take the one you have and pass it on and keep passing it forward. Regardless of what happens to me, remember the basic ideas presented here and never be afraid to ask 'why,' or 'why not?' It all reminds me of a time, a very long time ago when a bunch of guys got together to sign a document... a very dangerous document that could have gotten them all hanged. It ended with the words: "We mutually pledge to each other our lives, our fortunes, and our sacred honor..." And then one guy got up, picked up the pen and signed his name in really big letters. Consider that now done, and follow...

End Warning: The masses don't ask for much, decent food, a roof that doesn't leak and a chance to take the family to a ball game for an evening, or that Disney Vacation once a year while the kids are young. If our Representatives can't appreciate these values, and indeed, share in them, there will come a time when dissatisfaction has grown out of all control and everything else will be too little, too late. Congressmen, Senators, you need to be one of your people, not just 'responsible for them.' You need to find those things that get in the way of that perception and eliminate their influence, be it political parties, special interest groups or a lifestyle you were not born to.

Together, we all need to make America the Land of Opportunity again.

About the Author

Bruce Jenvey was raised in rural Michigan with a great interest in history and popular culture. After twenty years in the Detroit area working in the advertising industry, he founded *Great Lakes Cruiser Magazine* and spent the next decade traveling the region as both historian and journalist. In the years after 9/11, he turned his efforts toward fiction, writing four novels and several shorter works.

Today, Bruce is the award-winning author of *Angela's Coven,* and *My Father's Ashes* as well as other works of interest and is enjoying his retirement in small town Michigan.

www.facebook.com/CovenBooks

Made in the
USA
Monee, IL